Global Communication and Misunderstandings

An Exploratory Study of Interpersonal Relationships, Management, Business Negotiations and Promotional Marketing in Diverse Cultural Settings.

Bagher Fardanesh, Ph.D.

INFI∞ITY
PUBLISHING.COM

Copyright © 2009 by Bagher Fardanesh

ISBN 0-7414-5341-X

Published by:

PUBLISHING.COM

1094 New DeHaven Street, Suite 100
West Conshohocken, PA 19428-2713
Info@buybooksontheweb.com
www.buybooksontheweb.com
Toll-free (877) BUY BOOK
Local Phone (610) 941-9999
Fax (610) 941-9959

Printed in the United States of America

Published September 2009

Dedicated to Soheila, Tooca, and Taara

Preface

Our reliance on interpersonal and corporate communication is an increasingly fast-paced trend. One reason for this trend is the technological advancements in communication, such as the Internet and teleconferencing, which facilitate sending and receiving messages. The other reason is the need for more communication, brought on by economic integrations, outsourcing, and the expansion of world trade, mainly because of the emerging markets, to name a few.

Expectedly, more communication leads the way to misunderstanding or to being misunderstood. I am writing this book considering how a simple misunderstanding could create severe consequences. Misunderstanding has no boundaries, as for instance, it can occur between friends, co-workers, and business negotiators. Misunderstanding, as I will explain, is more apparent in international settings because of diversity of customs, protocols, perceptions, and languages.

The purpose of this book is to provide further awareness of many situations and types of misunderstandings, both within and in cross-cultural settings, focusing on interpersonal, management, marketing, and business communication. By taking into account various unwanted and irrevocable outcomes of misunderstandings, I will conclude with a host of guidelines for minimizing such conditions for misunderstanding.

My hope is to contribute by promoting shared understanding among all in our culturally diverse environment.

In this book I use the term "misunderstanding" in a very general way that includes the formation of intentional or unintentional ambiguity and the giving of misleading information. Another important note to the reader is that a range of cultures and customs will be reviewed merely on a comparative basis with no intention of being judgmental. For this matter, I apologize in advance for any inadvertent shortcoming on my part.

Acknowledgments

In writing the last page, the acknowledgments, several people come effortlessly to my mind who were instrumental in the completion of my work.

I want to thank my long-time friend, Dr. Honaid Vasi, MD, as I have benefited from his wisdom and knowledge in the field of psychology. Equally, I am thankful to my friend and colleague, Professor Denis Kaplan, for reviewing my book and keenly sharing his invaluable insights. I would also like to express my gratitude to my friend Mr. Mathew Esworthy for his guidance and input.

My sincere appreciation goes to Ms. Shana Gass, the reference librarian at Towson University who proactively provided me with pertinent literature. I would like to extend my appreciation to Ms. Courtney Kinpp and Ms. Elaine Andrews for editing my work.

I would like to thank many of my colleagues in the fields of business, marketing, management, international relations, and organizational development for sharing their views and for their guidance toward the development of this book.

These acknowledgments would not be complete without thanking my two daughters, Tooca and Taara, who read my manuscript and gave me constructive input. I am mostly indebted to my wife, Soheila, for her unflinching support and encouragements.

Table of Contents

PREFACE   i

ACKNOWLEDGMENTS   iii

CHAPTER ONE: THE NATURE, PURPOSE, AND
PROCESS OF COMMUNICATION   1

    A Growing Trend of Human Communication   3

    How Do We Communicate?   6

    Why Do We Communicate?   7

    Handle It with Care   11

    What Is Ahead?   13

    Endnotes   14

    Recommended Reading   14

CHAPTER TWO: TAKING A TOUR IN THE FIELD OF
VERBAL AND NONVERBAL COMMUNICATION   17

    Understanding and Its Related Categories   17

    Verbal Explicit and Implicit Communication   21

    Nonverbal Communication   23

    Final Notes   28

    Endnotes   29

    Recommended Reading   29

CHAPTER THREE: THE MANY FACES OF
MISUNDERSTANDINGS   31

    Unintentional Misunderstandings   32

    Misunderstanding and Disaster   36

    Same Culture, Different Understanding   37

    Colloquialisms, Jargons, and Acronyms   39

    My Misunderstandings   42

Intentional Misunderstanding 45
Final Notes 48
Endnotes 50
Recommended Reading 50

CHAPTER FOUR: MANAGEMENT AND
COMMUNICATION IN COMPLEX ORGANIZATIONS 52
Employment: Interview and Evaluation 54
Playing Politics 58
Interacting with Employees: A Matter of
Inconsistency 59
Variation of Personality in the Workplace 62
Customer Satisfaction 63
Management Effectiveness 69
Final Notes 75
Endnotes 76
Recommended Reading 76

CHAPTER FIVE: MARKETING AMBIGUITY 79
An Overview of Marketing Evolution in
the United States 79
Encountering the Unexpected 84
Unintentional Ambiguity in Marketing 90
Commercials 92
Per Capita Income and Level of Literacy 95
Concluding Points 96
Endnotes 97
Recommended Reading 97

CHAPTER SIX: GLOBAL NEGOTIATIONS,
PROTOCOLS, AND MARKET ENTRY 99
The Two Broad Categories of Negotiation 100
No Room for Negotiation 106
Instrumentality and Terminality of
Negotiation 109

Diverse Protocols and Beyond   111
Misunderstanding in Global Market Entry   115
Marketing Research   117
Final Notes   118
Endnotes   120
Recommended Reading   120

CHAPTER SEVEN: CONDITIONS AND
COMMUNICATION   121
Luckily It Did Not Happen   122
Self-Misunderstanding   125
Organizations and Cultural Diversity   127
Problematic Facilitators: Words and
Phrases   129
The Intricacy of Communication in
Cross-Cultural Settings   132
Tackling Communication in Cross-Cultural
Settings   135
Final Notes   137
Endnotes   138
Recommended Reading   138

EXHIBITS
4.1 Determinants of Managerial
Effectiveness   74
5.1 A Conceptual Gap Between the Supply
of and the Demand for Goods and Services
During the Evolution of Marketing in the
United States: Stages of Marketing
Development   83

CHAPTER ONE

THE NATURE, PURPOSE, AND PROCESS OF COMMUNICATION

Yu, an exchange student from China, came to the United States to pursue her education at one of the well-known universities of the East Coast. Her objective was to earn a B.S. degree in Business Administration. In one of the required courses in which she was enrolled, the instructor assigned 20 out of 100 points for class participation toward the final grade.

Yu had done an excellent job on her exams and quizzes in class, but she fell short in class participation and asking questions. It appeared that she had a strong background in mathematics and, therefore, she didn't take the course seriously enough to engage in class discussions. Subsequently, she received a low mark in this part of the evaluation, which affected her final grade.

Her low class participation was not because of lack of interest in this class; rather, it was because of two notable reasons: First, Yu was fluent in the English language, but she had an accent, which made her feel uncomfortable speaking in front of others in class. Second, in Chinese culture, a high level of respect is placed on the elderly and those of higher authority. With this consideration, when instructions or assignments are given by the teacher, students typically follow them, instead of questioning them. In short, Yu received a lower final grade because she wanted to recognize and respect the authority of her professor. This is a case of simple misunderstanding, whereby a behavior with good intentions was interpreted differently.

Speaking of classrooms, in some schooling systems or cultures, it is customary for students to stand up when their instructor walks into the classroom. The professor then gives the students permission to sit down. At Boulder High School, there was a student who stood up for the instructor while other students were seated. The instructor could not understand why this student stood in the middle of the classroom until I had a chance to explain.

When I was a student, I felt uncomfortable as my professor was sitting behind me while listening to students' presentations because I felt it was impolite to show my back to a professor. In these instances I would turn my chair sideways. Some of my professors could not figure out my repositioning. Today, I see that some of my students are doing exactly the same for me, and I simply thank them.

Misunderstandings derive from verbal and nonverbal communications on a limitless basis. They may occur among friends and families, within corporations, in governmental settings, and in domestic to multinational organizations. In short, whenever there is human interaction, there is a potential for misunderstandings and communication breakdowns.

A Growing Trend of Human Communication

It is quite difficult, if not impossible, to quantify the rate of growth in human communications. However, the following three perspectives display the enormity of communication: national, organizational, and interpersonal.

National Perspective Clusters of countries in a given region, commonly known as regional economic integrations, have been formed notably for the minimizing or eliminating of tariffs, quotas, and such similar measures among the member countries. Economic integration is geared toward providing economic cooperation, synergy, and a higher level of competitiveness in the world market. A basic form of such integration is the Free Trade Area (FTA), such as the North American Free Trade Agreement (NAFTA), which comprises Canada, the United States, and Mexico; the European Free Trade Association (EFTA) also functions under FTA agreement and consists of Iceland, Liechtenstein, Norway, and Switzerland. (In this form of integration, generally, there is free trade among the member countries. However, each member sets its own trade policies toward nonmember countries.)

Organizational Perspective Increasing numbers of organizations that have been faced with the pressure of intraindustry competition are

3

taking the initiative by going to other countries to seek new markets for their goods and services. These corporations select one or more types of entry in foreign markets, including exports, franchising, management contract, contract manufacturing, turnkey operation, or strategic alliance. For example, Kodak, which entered Japan's market through a fully owned subsidiary, and Toyota and General Motors (GM), which through joint-venture agreement are manufacturing automobile engines. Their jointly formed company is the United Motor Manufacturing, Inc. in California.

Another reason for going international is to take advantage of certain opportunities that might not be available domestically; for example, the low cost of production, less restrictive laws and regulations for their operations, and tax incentives that are offered by some developing countries to attract foreign investments.

A pertinent point is the remarkable growth in foreign direct investment (FDI) within the past twenty years or so. In 1985, FDI amounted to 57 billion dollars. In 2006, FDI has increased to more than 1.352 trillion dollars.[1] The expansion of emerging markets such as in China, India, South Korea, South Africa, and Brazil seems to suggest that corporate involvement in the international arena will continue to grow on a long-term basis.

Individual Perspective Modern and technologically advanced means of transportation, such as jetliners and high-speed trains, have facilitated international travel. Also, we can look at the overall rate of increase in per capita income worldwide as another condition for the expansion of travel.

There are a number of reasons for people to go from one country to another; commonly, to pursue higher education in a selected field of study, to further career opportunities, or to become an expatriate fulfilling an organizational mission. Also, individuals travel across national borders to acquire more knowledge about other cultures and customs, or simply to travel for its excitement.

Expansion of Communication Channels

Not long ago, who could have imagined an airplane carrying over 500 passengers from one corner of the world to another or that such carriers would come with bedrooms, private cabins, and social gathering and shopping areas. This exactly describes the newly made Airbus A380. As the Associated Press reported, Emirate Airlines has ordered 245 new wide-body airplanes, 58 of which will be A380 super jumbo jets.[2]

In addition to such expansion, there have been impressive advances in telecommunication. I remember that twenty years ago or so, calling overseas was often an annoying experience. The caller had to contact the telephone company, requesting to speak with an overseas operator. The overseas operator would collect necessary information from the caller, including the phone numbers of the other party overseas. Later that day or the next day, the operator would have contacted the caller, stating that the party was on the line. If there was a disconnection, which was not unusual, the caller had to go through the same process again. Now, we can dial directly to almost anywhere in the world, even with our cell phones.

Rotary telephones, typewriters, telegraphs, and telexes have given way to facsimile machines, touch-tone phones, e-mails, cell phones, text messages, video conferences, virtual social networking, and more. These technological developments have paved the way for more communication among individuals within and between countries.

The need for communication on national, organizational, and personal levels, along with more efficient and effective means of communication, has dramatically increased human contact. Concurrent to these developments, there has been a growing trend in misunderstandings, particularly when communication occurs among people with different languages, dialogues, and customs.

How Do We Communicate?

A typical communication process consists of several distinct but highly interdependent steps, which are as follows:

The Initial Communicator is someone with a need or preference to communicate with another party. The initiator converts the intended thoughts and feelings into a message, which is known as the encoding or formation of a message. The message then is conveyed to the other party through a channel such as an e-mail, a cell phone call, or simply the air, in the case of face-to-face communication.

The Receiver is the party who decodes the received message (who understands the message). The receiver of the message subsequently sends a response back to the initial communicator. The response, for example, could be:

"I agree, and I will do it..."

"I understand what you are saying, but I don't agree with it ..." or

"I am not sure what you are telling me...."

Based on one of these responses, the initial communicator may compose and send another message. The question is: Could the receiver of a message refuse to give any type of response to the initial communicator? The answer is likely to be no, because no response is a response (feedback) in itself, particularly in a face-to- face communication.

Noise is often noticed in interpersonal communications. The meaning of the word "noise" is not limited to a sound that is present in the middle of a communication. A noise can be defined as any environmental or behavioral condition that impedes or interferes with effective communication. For someone who is walking near a busy intersection, noise can impede a clear conversation. A lecturer who often pounds on the podium with a pen or keeps pacing the classroom may distract students from the lecture, which would be another example of noise.

Why Do We Communicate?

We communicate for a variety of reasons. From a broad perspective, we rely on interpersonal communication to facilitate socialization as well as to perform tasks and functions. Below, they will be discussed in some detail.

Communication as a Social Satisfier

fier Imagine that Jill just entered her newly rented apartment and must wait for a few hours for the new furniture to be delivered. The place is empty, with no telephones, television, radio, or any means of communication. Or suppose that Donald wanted to be the first in line to enter a bank to see a loan officer. He arrived at the bank quite early and had to wait in the hallway for the bank to open. These two individuals may have something in common. They may keep looking at their watches to see how time is dragging itself from one minute to another. That would be an annoying and unpleasant experience for them.

In one of my recent graduate classes, the topic was employment satisfaction. One of the students, Bill, stated that he was unhappy with his job and was looking for a better one. Several students probed the cause of his dissatisfaction: Inconvenient hours? Not enough working space? Unreasonable expectations of the immediate superior? A long commute? Low pay? Many deadlines to meet? The answer was "no" to all of the above.

He was working in a governmental agency where there was almost nothing for him to do. Every week he had to sign off on a few similar or repetitive reports, and there was hardly any human interaction during his working hours.

One of our basic needs is to socialize.[3] To be deprived of it causes life to be dull, boring, and uninspiring. This is where interpersonal communication comes to the rescue, as it acts as a bridge between our social needs and satisfaction.

Through socialization we are able to share our feelings, experiences, intentions, and knowledge.

Additionally, it is an opportunity to monitor the way we relate ourselves to others and make appropriate adjustments as needed. This reminds me of an old saga, which is worth mentioning here.

There was a man named Hakim, who was a role model for many because of his manner, his courtesy, and the way he cared for others. Someone who was very impressed by Hakim could not keep himself from asking him a question. He asked Hakim, "How did you learn to become so well mannered, courteous, and kind?" Hakim paused and then responded, "It was simple, I learned it from those who were not very well mannered, courteous, and kind."

Tasks and Functions Facilitator

One afternoon, on a busy street in Baltimore, I was waiting for a taxi cab. In a few moments a taxi arrived and I entered. As usual, the driver asked for the address. I noticed my hoarse voice as a result of a cold that I had just recovered from. Luckily, the understanding driver handed me a piece of paper for me to write down the address. If I couldn't write or if he couldn't read, I would have had a hard time getting to my destination.

It was only a few days ago that I was in a department store, where I was at the counter to pay for a pair of gloves. A customer approached the counter and asked for "sears." An associate at the counter gave the direction to the Sears department store in the mall. The customer interrupted her and said, "I am not asking for the Sears store, but I am asking for sears." At that time we were not sure of the man's intention. He said to the associate, "You know, I am looking for the drapes." Apparently the customer wanted "sheers," but because of his accent, it was difficult for him to pronounce the sound "sh."

We depend on communication for our everyday activities, yet it is frequently susceptible to many unexpected conditions that hinder its effectiveness. Within an organizational setting, we also rely on communication in different ways, which include the following. Downward communication signifies communication from a manager or superior to an employee. It is frequently for the purpose of giving instructions, assignments, or performance evaluations. The next is upward communication, which refers to communication initiated by employees to superiors, to report their work progress, ask for guidance, or share any conflicts or problems that may affect completion of their assigned tasks. Aside from upward and downward communication, there is lateral communication through which managers of the same hierarchical level communicate with each other mainly for the purpose of collaboration and coordination of workflow and resources.

Furthermore, the top manager communicates with the board of directors on a periodic basis to report overall organizational standing and performance, and to receive recommendations. It should be mentioned that communicating with the stakeholders is considered a high priority for the top management. It means communication with those entities, such as community, government, and stockholders, which have a certain level of concern or interest regarding the organization.

Ceremonial Communication In a situation such as a job interview, communication commonly takes place conscientiously and with thoughtfulness. However, more than seldom, messages or feedbacks are given on a ceremonial or assumptive basis.

You have probably experienced someone calling you to ask, "How are you doing?" Without any pause for your response, the caller usually goes on to the intended message. When leaving a social gathering, you may say to another guest, "It was good to meet you; hope to see you soon." The guest may say "Yes, you too." The response is based on the assumption that you have said "Take care," or something similar.

Intellectual Competence Occasionally, I have come across a question of concern from my students. They want to know what benefits come with learning so many things, such as mathematical calculations or statistical formulations that they will probably never see or use again. My response is that, at the very least, they are exercise for the mind. For example, class and group discussions on such topics will enhance our reasoning ability and learning experience. Such exercises will help us with our comprehension and problem solving ability. I continue to say that it is like those who perform physical exercise over time. They are more likely to develop stronger and fitter bodies compared with those who do not. At Michigan University, Oscar Ybarra, a professor of psychology, and his team conducted an interesting and extensive study. The outcome of their study suggests that socialization and discussions help to enhance "mental function."[4]

Handle It with Care

A message can be changed, added, or deleted before its transmission, but once it is sent and decoded by the receiver, it becomes too late to erase it. Therefore, the message should be handled with care; otherwise, it may end up with unwanted consequences.

According to a Chinese proverb, "We get sick from what we put in our mouths, but we get injured by what comes out of our mouths."[5]

The following is a story of a lumberjack and a lion that demonstrates this consequence.[6]

Once upon a time, deep in a forest, there was a lumberjack who had a lion friend. One day walking in the forest, he saw his lion friend and decided to invite him to his home for supper. The lion gladly accepted the lumberjack's invitation. That evening, at the dinner table, the lumberjack was annoyed by the way the lion was gulping the food. In the middle of supper, the lumberjack couldn't keep himself from making a provocative remark about the lion's table manners. The lion paused, then asked the man to pick up his axe and hit him on the head. The confused man, with a quivering voice, responded, "But, why?" The lion threatened the man's life if he didn't follow the order. Reluctantly, out of fear for his life, the lumberjack followed the lion's order by hitting the lion's head with the axe. The lion didn't say a word, and walked away with a bleeding head.

Several years passed until one day the lumberjack and the lion met each other eye to eye. The man was excited to see the lion, but still remembered the incident of that evening. After the usual greeting, the lumberjack with hesitancy asked the lion about his injury. The lion said, "First, let's see if you can find the spot where you hit me." The man looked at the lion's head very closely, but could not see any scars.

The lion then declared rather sadly, "Although there is no trace of injury or pain from your axe, the pain of your words of humiliation is still with me, as your words were sharper than the edge of your iron axe."

What Is Ahead?

Human activities and interactions take place in so many different places and situations, such as social gatherings, international business negotiations, employment interviews, marketing and buying decisions, and so on. With this consideration, this book is about the many misunderstandings and ambiguities associated with verbal and nonverbal communication within and among cultures. Also, it provides potential guidelines for more effective communication.

Communication of some sort is present in every aspect of our lives, and therefore it leaves much potential for misunderstanding. With all good intentions between the communicators, misunderstanding and ambiguity can occur particularly in international settings. This is because of a multitude of languages, customs, and cultural backgrounds. In the following chapters, I will differentiate between verbal and nonverbal communication, and discuss how each could lead to misunderstandings if they are not handled with care.

Communication and misunderstanding will be elaborated in several domains, which include interpersonal, organizational management, transportation, international marketing and promotional strategies, and intercultural business negotiations. Furthermore, a set of general guidelines will be given to enhance effective communication within and between cultures.

ENDNOTES

1. World Bank, *World Development Indicators database*, http://www.worldbank.org/query.

2. Aziz Shah, *Associated Press*, "Arab airline plans huge order fleet," in *The Baltimore Sun*, January 3, 2008, p.2D.

3. See Abraham H. Maslow, "A Theory of Human Motivation," *Psychological Review, 50, 1943, pp.370-396.* This theory provides a detailed explanation and hierarchy of human needs. Maslow's hierarchy of needs is notably popular, and can be found in many textbooks of various fields, including management, organizational behavior, psychology, sociology, marketing, consumer behavior, and advertising.

4. Oscar Ybarra, "Idle Chatter? Hardly," *Los Angeles Times*, November 5, 2007, a. Part F. p.2.

5. Roger E. Axtell, *The Do's and Taboos of International Trade: a Small Business Primer,* Revised ed. (New York: John Wiley & Sons, 1994), p. 216.

6. An old story, which was discussed in one of my high school classes.

RECOMMENDED READING

Ashley Montagu. *Touching: The Human Significance of the Skin.* New York: Columbia University Press, 1971.

Lillian H. Chaney and Jeanette S. Martin. *Intercultural Business Communication*. Upper Saddle River, NJ: Prentice Hall, 2000.

Paul Watzlawick, Janet H. Beavin, and Don D. Jackson. *Pragmatics of Human Communication*. New York: W.W. Norton, 1967.

Rudolph F. Verderber. *Communicate*. Belmont, CA: Wadsworth, 1993.

Stanley Schachter. *The Psychology of Affiliation: Experimental Studies of the Sources of Gregariousness*. Stanford University Press: Stanford, 1968.

CHAPTER TWO

TAKING A TOUR IN THE FIELD OF VERBAL AND NONVERBAL COMMUNICATION

The purpose of this chapter is to examine the concept of understanding and lack of it, and also to differentiate between explicit and implicit verbal communication by explaining how the crossroads between them tend to create ambiguity and communication breakdown. Furthermore, this chapter discusses the many forms of nonverbal communication and its potential for misunderstandings, particularly in diverse cultural settings.

Understanding and Its Related Categories

Understanding Suppose a manager gives one of his employees an assignment with a designated due date. The job is done accordingly and submitted to the manager on time. This indicates that the employee received the message as intended by the manager. Clear understandings between the communicators are commonly known as effective communications.

Not Understanding This is when the receiver of a message is not clear on the purpose and content of the message. This can be result of many conditions, such as when the sender of the message speaks rapidly or in a low voice, or when the receiver is not paying attention to what is being communicated.

Misunderstanding Misunderstanding takes place when there is a discrepancy between the content of a message that is sent and its interpretation by the receiver. Misunderstanding is the source of many unwanted outcomes in interpersonal interactions. It can break friendships, family ties, and put an end to business negotiations. Misunderstandings can even result in a loss of human lives, as will be shown later in this chapter. There was a recent case caused by misunderstanding which was brought before a small claims court judge. A buyer of household furniture (plaintiff) claimed that the salesperson (defendant) promised to let her have a sofa for free after buying the whole living room set. The salesperson stressed that while they were negotiating the price of a chair, he said to the buyer that she could have the sofa at the same price, meaning the same price as the chair, not one price for both items. The judge determined that this was a case of misunderstanding. He ruled that the buyer either pay the same price for the sofa as she did for the chair, or return the sofa to the seller.

Imitated Understanding There are situations in which the receiver of a message does not (fully) understand what is being communicated, but prefers to demonstrate understanding. A manager gives a procedural instruction to a group of employees and asks them if anyone needs further explanation. Suppose an employee did not understand the instruction, but did not ask for further clarification. It could have been because the employee felt uncomfortable asking questions because presumably others did understand.

During a lecture, a student could pretend understanding by showing attentiveness, although the student is thinking of something else.

Imitate Not Understanding In many cases the receiver of a message pretends lack of understanding of what is being said. For example, in the case of a dispute, one person may say to the other, "I don't understand what you are talking about," when indeed the message is fully understood. The repetition of the same message may give the other party more time to come up with a better response.

There are many forms of misunderstanding, as we will review in the upcoming chapters. However, the focus here is on misunderstandings relevant to the study of verbal explicit-direct and verbal implicit-indirect interpersonal communication. This chapter will also cover the nature and importance of non-verbal communication, as well as potential misunderstandings pertinent to this form of interpersonal communication.

One of my friends, Alfred, shared this experience with me. He said that one of his relatives, who lives overseas, once called him requesting to borrow

$2500.00 by explaining the urgency of the matter. The relative promised to pay back the sum within one month. Alfred hesitantly agreed to his relative's request and sent the money. Alfred waited for about six weeks without hearing from the borrower. My friend explained that he has had his relative on the phone several times since then. He pointed out that when he talked about anything but the borrowed money, they had a perfect phone connection. However, the moment he started asking him for the $2,500, his relative suddenly began to experience a very bad phone connection with him and could not understand what was being said.

Action-Reaction Dynamics of Misunderstanding There are cases in which a comment leads to increasing misunderstanding. This can happen *vertically,* by which I mean augmented misunderstanding between two parties. *Laterally* is a condition of (probable) misunderstanding between two individuals, then, a third party intervenes.

A Case of Vertical Misunderstanding Mr. F. is an active member at a professional association who usually shows up to the meetings wearing the latest style suits and designer ties. At one of the meetings, Mr. F. arrived a few minutes late with an uncommonly casual outfit. Another member, Mr. B., as an ice-breaking device, commented, "What happened to your tie? You forgot to wear it?" The misunderstanding was that Mr. F. thought this comment in the presence of others was a way to remind him that he needs to have a professional look for all meetings. Mr. F. then expected some type of reaction. In the next meeting, Mr. F. was unfriendly toward Mr. B. During that meeting, in a subtle manner, Mr. F. made remarks on the lack of validity of some of the points Mr. B was making. Mr. B., unaware of the motive for this member's behavior, decided to react as well. This misunderstanding manifested itself in an action- reaction loop that affected their professional relationship. Therefore, it is crucial to be cognizant of multiple dimensions of communication breakdown as a result of verbal and nonverbal communication. Equally important is to avoid falling into the loop of action-reaction in such a way that it deepens the existing misunderstanding in interpersonal communication.

A Case of Horizontal Misunderstanding John was an employee of a local electrical company. He was known for using others' electrical tools without permission.

One early afternoon, one of John's co-workers, Mike, was looking for his drill when he noticed John was using it. An argument erupted between the two in the presence of another co-worker, Tony. The argument continued between John and Mike, until Tony said, "Mike, just let it go, it is not worth it," meaning John did not want to understand or admit his wrong behavior. Mike, who misunderstood this comment, became even more annoyed and expanded his argument to include Tony, saying, "What do you mean by 'let it go'? If someone did this to you, wouldn't you react the same way?"

Verbal Explicit and Implicit Communication

Effective use of implicit and explicit communication is quite situational, and is a function of many factors, some of which are indicated below.

- The cultural settings and individual attitudes, perceptions, and expectations through which interpersonal communication take place.

- The organizational or corporate culture within which employees interact.

- One's comfort zone and habits of using direct and indirect communication.

- The level of understanding, friendship, and cooperation among the communicators.

- The nature and the content of the message that needs to be communicated

- The urgency of communication

- The importance of saving face and maintaining harmony in interpersonal relationships.

Explicit or Implicit Communication Is a Matter of Choice.

The sender of a message is in charge of deciding to rely on explicit or implicit communication. The following are two examples that show both types of communication.

While I was student at the University of Colorado, one of the emeritus professors, Dr. N., was diagnosed with cancer. A University administrator and I volunteered to drive Dr. N. once a week from Boulder to Denver for cancer treatments. One day, after the treatment was administered, the physician asked Dr. N. and me to wait in his office. I needed to be there to assist him to walk. The physician looked at some charts and documents, and then he said explicitly to Dr. N. that he had about two more months to live. Dr. N. seemed to have difficulty believing what he had just heard. He then turned his head toward me and asked me to repeat the physician's comment. Saddened by the news and with hesitancy, I started my euphemistic[1] version, during which I was interrupted by the physician, who repeated his earlier pronouncement. Dr. N. was so distraught by the news, he almost fainted.

A few years back, in one of my business classes, I handed out the students' midterm exams, which I had graded. At the end of the class period, one of my students came to me with her exam. Politely, she asked if I could further explain the answer to one of the questions on the exam. While looking at the question, I noticed that inadvertently I had not given her points for the correct answer to that specific question. Implicit communication had directed my attention to the answer with the missing points.

Nonverbal Communication

Nonverbal communication is a resourceful way to send or receive messages. Peter Drucker, who is known as the father of modern management, had noted that "The most important thing in communication is to hear what isn't being said."[2]

Verbal communication is limited to spoken and written forms, but there are many types of nonverbal cues, including facial expressions, gestures, selection of color and style of clothing, overall physical appearance, handshakes, tone of voice, and manners, to name a few. Nonverbal communication has considerably more potential for misunderstandings.

In this section of the chapter, I will describe a few types of nonverbal communication as related to ambiguity and misinterpretations.

Facial Expression and Nodding An important part of nonverbal communication is facial, which enriches verbal communication because of its ability to signal many messages, such as happiness, surprise, confusion, shame, fear, or frustration, to name a few.

Many instructors who are teaching asynchronous-time independent courses assert that because they are unable to see the facial reactions of their students while teaching, it is difficult to know which point should be repeated or reemphasized. In this regard, one of my colleagues who teaches mathematics courses online pointed out that the number of students who fail his online courses is clearly higher than the failure rate in traditional classroom settings.

Another example of facial expression is nodding, which often replaces or supports the word "yes" or "no." The interpretation of nodding is not the same among all cultures, which may result in misunderstanding. In North America, vertical movement of the head commonly signifies "yes" or agreement with what has been conveyed. On the other hand, in some parts of India, horizontal movement of the head is used to send similar messages.

Some years ago I went to a casual Indian restaurant in Takoma Park, Maryland, for carry-out lunch. When it was my turn to order, I asked for a dozen samosas. The restaurant was very busy and it was sometimes hard to communicate with the person across the counter. I was asked if I wanted frozen samosas. In response, I relied on my nonverbal communication by moving my head horizontally, meaning "no." But it was understood as "yes." Later I found that all of my samosas were frozen.

Many management, communication, and professional development training programs refer to the importance of eye contact. However, it should be noted that its importance varies across cultural settings. In China, Japan, and many South American countries, for instance, eye contact is de-emphasized. A few years ago, the manager of a clothing store dismissed one of the sales associates. The reason given was that, "He never wanted to make eye contact with me. I knew that he was hiding something from me, which made me very concerned and uncomfortable." Later on, the manager found that the sales associate who tried to avoid eye contact did it out of respect for his superior.

Fingers Our fingers are major sources of wordless communication. They are usually used to show facts, whereas facial expressions mainly display feelings and emotions.

Each day, there may be many occasions in which we rely on our fingers as a reliable source to communicate with others. They are used to indicate direction, such as showing the shortest distance on a map. Fingers are also used to indicate numerical value. Consider a crowded movie theater line. We might use our fingers to show the number of tickets we want to purchase.

Fingers are also used to indicate selections. Think of choosing ice cream with a specific flavor when communicating with the person behind the counter. In other situations, some speakers tend to bring all the fingers of one hand together to create a fist and tap it on the podium to emphasize a point.

Careful usage of fingers is important to minimizing misunderstandings, notably in multifaceted cultural settings. A server might ask a guest in a restaurant,

"How is your food?" While eating, the guest might form a circle by connecting his thumb and index finger to indicate that the food is sumptuous. This formation of circle, however, does not have the same meaning in every country. For example, it is a vulgar sign in Pakistan or Turkey.

In the United States during the late 60s and early 70s, raising both the index and middle finger to create a "V" shape became a popular gesture, symbolizing peace and friendship. Although this tends to have a somewhat universal meaning, in some countries it still translates to an offensive gesture.

Colorful Cultures Colors are another significant means of unwritten and unspoken communication that we rely on. The following are a few illustrations of their uses.

Means of Guidance When entering a hospital, often in front of the information desk, there are several lines on the floor, each with a distinct color that guides visitors to their desired unit, such as emergency or intensive care. To follow a colored designated walkway to a specific unit is less confusing and simpler than looking at a map. There are more situations in which colors are used to indicate directions, such as in metro stations.

Another use of color is to facilitate the flow of traffic on the roads and minimize accidents. Traffic lights at intersections, yield signs, and railroad crossing signs are a few examples of its importance.

Meaning and Interpretation of Colors In terms of meaning and interpretation, colors are not immune to misunderstandings. In the United States, the color green symbolizes prosperity and growth, as well as concern for nature. For instance, the term "green marketing" denotes production and other marketing activities performed in an environmentally responsible manner. The interpretation of this color may not be the same across cultures. In this regard, let us consider the following multiple choice questions.

1. In which country is the color green associated with danger and disease?

   a. Guatemala
   b. Mali
   c. Malaysia
   d. Switzerland

2. In Western Europe, purple is the color of prestige and grandeur, but in various parts of _____, it symbolizes death or mourning.

   a. The Middle East
   b. The Far East
   c. Africa
   d. South America

3. In _____, avoid offering gifts with white ribbon, as it is the color of death and mourning.

   a. Japan
   b. Bolivia
   c. Finland
   d. Italy

4. Yellow roses may symbolize sadness and despair in some parts of _____.

   a. Western Europe
   b. The Middle East
   c. North America
   d. Australia

5. Red is the color of joy and good luck in
   _____.

   a. China
   b. Pakistan
   c. Turkey
   d. Greece

6. Brown, tar-colored teeth in some parts of
   _____ are a sign of sophistication and
   wealth.

   a. Australia
   b. Zambia
   c. Thailand
   d. New Zealand

The answers to the above questions are: 1.c, 2.d, 3.a, 4.b, 5.a., and 6.c. Selection of colors should be a matter of importance in international activities, notably in marketing mix strategies to avoid blunders and misunderstandings.

Final Notes

Nonverbal cues have a wider variation than verbal communication. Additionally, the extent of their usage and interpretations differ across nations. Nonverbal cues can stand alone as methods of conveying intended messages, or can be complementary to verbal communication in face-to-face situations. Considering various scenarios as described above, it becomes clear how simple it is for misunderstandings to arise.

ENDNOTES

1. Euphemism can be defined as the conveyance of unwanted news in a subtle and less direct manner to lessen its impact.

2. Peter F. Drucker, in an interview with Bill Moyers, *A World of Ideas* (New York: Doubleday, 1989), p. 408.

RECOMMENDED READING

Don Hellriegel and John W. Slocum, Jr. *Organizational Behavior.* Mason, OH: Thomson South-Western, 2007.

John J. Macionis. *Sociology.* Upper Saddle River, NJ: Pearson Prentice Hall, 2007.

Ronald B. Alder and George Rodman. *Understanding Human Communication.* Fort Worth, TX: Harcourt Brace College Publishers, 1994.

Tom D. Daniel and Barry K. Spiker. *Perspectives on Organizational Communication.* Madison, WI: WCB Brown and Benchmark, 1987.

William L. Gorden. *Communication: Personal and Public.* Sherman Oaks, CA: Alfred Publishing Company, 1978.

CHAPTER THREE

THE MANY FACES OF MISUNDERSTANDINGS

In this chapter I will present cases of misunderstanding resulting from verbal and non-verbal communication. These cases will illuminate a range of outcomes from misunderstanding and show the extent to which they can be catastrophic. There will be some references to acronyms, jargons, and colloquialisms as potential sources of misunderstandings. The chapter will include two personal cases of misunderstanding to describe how someone with good intentions can cause unwanted situations. Finally, I will explain that not all misunderstandings are unintentional. As we shall see, there are situations in which someone creates misunderstanding intentionally for one reason or another.

Unintentional Misunderstandings

In this section several cases of unintentional misunderstandings will be illustrated, some of which are verbal and nonverbal concurrently. In these unintentional misunderstandings you will find significant differences among conditions and outcomes. Two of these situations are the results of my own misunderstanding, which will be explained later in the chapter.

Don't Throw Away Those Matches! In the old days, in a remote small town, Joe, the owner of a grocery store, wanted to borrow money to expand his business. Since there were no financial institutions available in that town, borrowers were dependent on a few individual lenders. Joe heard of a generous man who had helped several business owners with their financial needs. By a previous arrangement, Joe went see the lender at his home. Right before ringing the bell, through the open windows, he heard the man telling someone: "Why are you wasting these few matches? Don't throw them away." Joe became hesitant to see the lender. After all, how generous could that man be if he was so concerned with a few matches? Despite his pessimism, Joe finally decided to go ahead and meet with the lender. This was an opportunity for Joe to explain his need for borrowing money for his grocery store. Shortly, an agreement was made between the two.

Before leaving, Joe hesitantly and curiously wanted to know how a generous man like the lender was also so frugal over a few matches. Joe finally asked the question. The lender, with a smile, replied, "I can see the misunderstanding caused by what I said about the matches and my willingness to help you out!" He continued by saying, "It is quite simple; if I were not a thrifty person, I would not have saved enough money to help others to expand their businesses."

Misunderstanding and the Term "As Usual"

Recently, the parents of one of my colleagues came from overseas to visit their son, Dr. H., at one of the well-known universities in Virginia. During their stay with their son, they were given a telephone card so they could call their extended family and friends in the United States. The parents also wanted to contact other friends and relatives overseas. Ms. H. asked her son whether they needed to use the calling card or whether they should call directly. Dr. H. said, "Simply dial as usual," meaning to use the calling card as she did before. But Ms. H. thought "as usual" meant calling overseas by direct dialing.

A few weeks later, Dr. H. received the "usual" bill from the telephone company, which was unusually high. The monthly payment that normally totaled around $100.00, this time amounted to almost $2500.00. Dr. H. who thought that there must have been a mistake at once contacted the telephone company and found there had been many hours of conversation from his telephone number to other countries. Luckily, Dr. H. explained the misunderstanding between himself and his parents regarding the term "as usual" and received a break on the bill.

A Case of Dry Cleaning

The wife of a CEO of an electronics corporation in Virginia wanted to send her expensive clothing and garments to the nearby, rather exclusive dry cleaner. For this, she instructed one of the maids to call the dry cleaner to come to the house and pick up a few bags of clothing. The maid immediately called the store with the instruction.

In the meantime, a not-for-profit organization called the house and asked for donations. Another maid happened to answer the phone. The maid who had a large amount of her own unwanted clothing happily agreed to donate it. She informed the caller that she would put the clothing in a few bags and leave them in front of the house for pickup. But she completely forgot to do so.

The next day, the truck for the not-for-profit organization arrived at the house. There were a few bags of clothing ready for dry cleaning and not for donation, which were inadvertently picked up by the not-for-profit organization.

Several days later, a maid in the house called the dry cleaner to find out when the clothing would be ready and delivered to the house. The manager of the store said that they came to the house for the pickup, but there was nothing to pick up.

Pointing the Finger One of my friends is a doctor of psychiatry who lives in Canada with his family. Recently, they spent their vacation in the United States, during which time they were invited to our home. His spouse had an experience concerning one of his psychiatric inpatients, which she shared with us.

One evening, while Mrs. N. and her husband were doing their grocery shopping, a middle-aged man smiled at her husband and walked toward them. Dr. N. then introduced the man to his wife. Mrs. N. thought he must have been one of her husband's colleagues, and as a result took a friendly approach to him. She said, "How are things going with you?" The man, a patient of Dr. N's, assumed that his doctor had already talked about him to Mrs. N. Therefore, the patient replied "Thanks to your husband, I am feeling much better and have no more problems with the law." Mrs. N., who was taken by surprise, said, "Well, I am very happy to hear that." At that time, mistakenly, the patient was confident that his psychiatrist had spoken about him with his wife or maybe even with some others as well. Soon after, the patient complained to the hospital that his psychiatrist had failed to keep the confidentiality of his patients, and requested that the hospital designate another psychiatrist for him.

Which Way to Look? In one of my graduate courses, we were discussing the challenges associated with nonverbal communication in international settings. One of these challenges was how the same behavior or signal could have different meanings because of cultural variations. In this regard one of my students shared her own experience with us.

Linda was working for an international airline company where she met a young man from Peru whom she later married. Now, they have a son named Mike who is six years old. Linda continued by saying that, like most Americans, she was accustomed to frequent eye contact with whomever she was communicating. She said that she was annoyed by her son, who would lean his head downward during their conversation, thus preventing eye contact. Linda then had to say, "Mike, I am not on the floor. Look at me when I am talking."

When her husband wanted to speak with Mike, it was another story. He was accustomed to having minimum eye contact in his conversation with others. He had already said several times to Mike that he should show some respect to his father by not looking at him.

Linda, furthermore, commented that one time both of them wanted to speak with Mike. As usual, she wanted him to make eye contact with her, and her husband wanted the opposite. Mike, who was confused and tired, in a witty way told them, "Why don't you two make up your mind as to what you want me to do: eye contact or no eye contact."

There are many cases of miscommunications with various outcomes, as David A. Ricks in his book *Blunders International Business* provided a series of such cases resulting from both verbal and nonverbal communications.[1]

Misunderstanding and Disaster

In aviation history, there have been many cases of jetliner crashes caused by some simple misunderstanding that ended with irrevocable, catastrophic results. The following are two such cases.

Running Out of Fuel On January 25, 1990, an Avianca Airlines Boeing 707 was en route to New York from Medellion, Colombia. While the jetliner circled in the air, waiting for clearance from the control tower to land at Kennedy International Airport, the level of fuel of the Boeing reached an alarmingly low level. The crew subsequently informed the tower of their low fuel level, but failed to convey the gravity of their condition. They should have reported "emergency" for priority landing. Shortly after, the plane crashed, resulting in 73 deaths.[2]

Two Jumbo Jets Collided Is it possible that a simple misunderstanding can lead to the loss of human lives? In March 27, 1977, at Tenerife airport in the Canary Islands, a KLM 747 jumbo jet slammed into a Pan American 747 jumbo jet. The latter jet was on the runway when the KLM jet was rushing toward it through heavy clouds, which created very poor visibility. The accident happened only a few seconds after the KLM jet's high speed takeoff. To avoid the collision with the Pan America jet liner on the runway, the KLM pilot tried to take off immediately, but fell short in altitude, resulting in the loss of more than 570 human lives.[3]

A joint report by KLM and Pan American airlines revealed that the major cause of the disaster was communication misunderstanding between the control tower and the KLM cockpit. The KLM co-pilot contacted the tower saying, "We are now at take off." The tower control, which had not yet cleared the plane for takeoff, considered the received message to mean, "We are now at takeoff position." Subsequently, the tower replied, "O.K...stand by for takeoff...I will call you." KLM was already speeding up, and it was too late for clarification.[4]

Same Culture, Different Understanding

Interpersonal communication with the use of the same language but at different wavelengths could also cause misunderstandings. A message can be encoded in a simple and clear way, but could reach the receiver without the same meaning. Divergent perceptions, experiences, and contexts are among many sources of miscommunication.

For example, Gerald Goldhaber reported that a film showed a manager who asked one of his employees to come up with a "model job," of his electrical-mechanical work, meaning doing an outstanding job. The employee misunderstood his manager and constructed a replica of his work. [5]

A Ceremonial Proposition One of the multinational corporations organized a welcoming event for its repatriates. The keynote speaker of the event was the vice president of the company who encouraged the repatriates to ask questions. At the end of his presentation, many hands were raised to ask questions. Oddly enough, it was evident that the speaker was reluctant to respond, as he gave very short and closed-ended answers. Subsequently, after a few responses, no one wanted to pose questions.

This experience suggests that soliciting questions from the audience is generally expected of speakers. However, some of them hope that no one would ask them any questions, fearing the possibility of being put on the spot. In this case, "Ask any questions" really meant, "Don't ask any questions." In other words, for some, such an offering is simply ceremonial and should not be taken in a literal fashion.

Misunderstanding of the Compliment or Well Wishes Have you been in a situation where you wanted to express your recognition or compliment someone because of that individual's superior performance, dedication, or creativity, but your expression somehow turned out to be more like a criticism? Or, simply you wanted to wish someone well, but it was interpreted as an ill wish? It seems that this type of misunderstanding occurs more than expected, particularly among people of different cultures.

In many Asians countries, being "fat" is the sign of being healthy because being meager or slim indicates malnourishment and sickness. Furthermore, being "fat" is a sign of being wealthy because an individual doesn't need to work and can afford to eat a lot.

A teenager who grew up in Western culture and was studying abroad went home to stay with her parents for the summer vacation. While there, at one point, her grandmother wished her to become "fat." The teenage daughter became irritated and was astounded at the comment.

Newstrom and Davis stated that a movie director commented to Joe, who was playing in a scene, that "Joe, you are doing one hell of a job." The comment was interpreted as a criticism which made Joe quite agitated.[6]

Colloquialisms, Jargons, and Acronyms

Colloquialisms, Jargons, and Acronyms are all major producers of misunderstandings, particularly in intercultural settings. Let us review some of them.

Colloquialism Colloquialism refers to a set of words composed in such an order that they carry a figurative meaning for people of a common culture.

"He bought a lemon" refers to purchasing a car with many mechanical problems.

"She was born with a silver spoon in her mouth" means that she was born into a wealthy family.

In France, when someone says, "Je n'ai pas froid aux yeaux" it means, "I am not afraid." However, it literally translates in english to "I do not have a cold in the eyes."

Jargon Various occupational fields have their own jargon or specialized terminology. This is to facilitate and expedite their communication. Jargon can be ambiguous to those outside of a specific field and can easily create miscommunication. For example, a governmental bureaucrat might say, "In this department there is a lot of red tape." This means that in the department there is an excessive amount of paperwork.

A financial broker might say, "This mutual fund is a no-load," which means the mutual fund has no sales charge. When someone says the market is "bearish," they are expressing pessimism about the market.

When a captain of a ship declares, "May Day," it means there is a distressing situation, an emergency.

The field of medicine has much jargon of its own. What do you think a "frequent flyer" is? If the answer is someone who travels by plane frequently then the answer is correct. However, this term in the medical field has a different meaning. It refers to a patient who comes to the emergency room frequently for unnecessary reasons.

A physician once mentioned that she sometimes has a difficult time communicating with her patients. She stated that the medical term "hypertension" means high blood pressure. Thus, when she uses this term, her patients might think of severe tension. Then she uses the common term, high blood pressure. However, this term needs further clarification for some of the patients from foreign countries because high blood pressure can often be mistaken for someone who has an extensive volume of blood in the body.

Acronyms There seems to be an endless number of acronyms. An acronym is a word that is composed of the first letters of other words. It is representative of more than one sequential word. Thus, acronyms are very efficient. Some of the well-known acronyms are IBM, which stands for International Business Machines, ASAP, which means "as soon as possible," and C.O.D., which stands for "cash on delivery."

An acronym can represent more than one combination of words and can therefore become subject to misunderstandings. In an emergency room, a patient overheard the nurse talking to the physician and referred to the patient as an S.O.B. As a result, the patient was quite upset, but did not reveal his feelings. Shortly after his release from the hospital, he wrote a letter of complaint to the management of the hospital, emphasizing that referring to a patient as an S.O.B. is offensive and unprofessional. After an investigation on the matter, the management promptly responded to this misunderstanding. They stated that S.O.B. is a common medical acronym that relates to patients who are "short of breath."

My Misunderstandings

The following two cases explain how my good intentions turned into misunderstanding. The first incident is from my high school years, and the second incident was caused by having different perceptions of protocols.

Following a Role Model too Closely Sometimes in our daily and common interactions with others, certain things happen with such impact that we may never forget them. The following incident of misunderstanding, for me, is one of them.

In my early high school years, I had a biology teacher, Mr. D., who was clearly my role model. I was always impressed by his manner, sophistication, attire, and his knowledge of the field. An interesting point about him was that often after a clear explanation of a topic, he used the expression, "Thus, it is now fully obvious."

I wanted to become like him, particularly after I finished my graduate education and entered into my professional life. I visualized Mr. D.'s behavior and comments in my mind. On occasion, when I was at home I practiced to be another Mr. D. I gradually felt that I was becoming a copy of my biology teacher. Not only was I walking like him when entering the classroom, but I also knew exactly at what point in his lecture he was going to use the expression, "Thus, it is now fully obvious." As a result, we started to say the term together.

The gross misunderstanding on my part was that I thought that Mr. D. and I now had a few things in common, whereas he thought I had the bad intention of mocking his behavior. One day, as usual, I entered the classroom imitating his manner of walking and sat in my seat. During his lecture and demonstration of the cells in the peel of an onion, as usual, he again relied on, "Thus, it is now fully obvious," which I said concurrently. Noting that I had done that repeatedly throughout the semester, Mr. D., whose patience with my behavior had reached its end, stopped lecturing. With his loudest voice, he shouted at me saying, "I am fed up with your mimicking behavior, and I want you immediately out of my class." The problem did not end there, as in my naïve mind I could not imagine his anger was directed toward me. I thought we were friends because of our commonalities, and I thought his comment was toward the student sitting behind me. I turned back to that student and said, "Don't you get it! Mr. D. wants you out of the classroom. What are you waiting for?" Again he thought I was trying to disturb the class by being funny. He shouted again while coming toward me, and said, "I am talking to you, and I mean you!" He went back to the podium, placed his books in his briefcase and rushed out of the classroom saying, "That's the end of it, as long as you come to this class."

The principal, who happened to be nearby, heard him. When he came to the classroom to find out what had happened, one of my classmates told him that Mr. D. suddenly became frustrated with me, put his books in his briefcase, and left the school.

As we have seen, the misunderstanding was that I was admiring my teacher, but I failed to transmit the message the way it was intended, and ultimately it was interpreted as my being disrespectful. After the clarification by my parents and my formal apology, I was readmitted to class.

Diversity of Protocol During my first few months at Colorado University, I was invited to a social event. I was asked by a friend if I could give a ride to another attendee because she preferred not to drive. I gladly accepted the request. That evening when we arrived at the event, I expected her to leave the automobile so I could lock the doors. On the other hand, she expected that I would get out and open the door for her. Unaware of her expectation, I asked her to open the door and exit the automobile, so I could lock the doors.

Later, through a mutual friend, I was told that she found me to be a sociable person, although with a shortcoming in my social protocol because of my not opening the automobile door for her. Of course, I learned what to do the next time.

Shortly after this experience, I found myself in a similar situation. As soon as I stopped the car, I opened the door on my side, went around the car, and gracefully opened the door for my passenger. I was expecting some kind of recognition, such as "thank you." Quite to the contrary! It was in the midst of the feminist movement, and she happened to be one of the proponents of the movement. She was truly offended by my opening the door for her. She declared something along the lines of, "Do you think I am not capable of opening the door, and I need your help?" I was unbearably confused because not opening the door for a woman was a problem, and opening the door for a woman was another problem.

A similar situation occurred when a young lady and I drove to an event. Arriving at our destination, I said to her, "Listen, with all due respect, do not ruin my evening, and please don't get upset, after all it is only a door." She was staring at me like I was out of my mind! I continued by saying, "If you want me to open the door for you, just tell me so. If you do not want me to open the door, simply say so. If you prefer to open the door for me for any reason, please feel free to do so." She was quite confused by my concern for who should open the door. She politely said, "Why does opening the door seem to be an issue for you?" I said, "Believe me, if you went through what I have been through, you would say the same thing." Later, I explained my experiences to her, and she could not stop laughing.

Intentional Misunderstanding

Interestingly, misunderstandings are more than seldom intentional. They are a way to create confusion for different reasons, as we will see. They can occur within an organization between a manager and employees or between an organization and customers. They can also happen on an interpersonal level.

Ambiguity of Department Policy

Robin was a software specialist in a large technology corporation. In one of the departmental meetings, the head of the department mentioned the importance of a dress code. Robin asked if wearing blue jeans was allowed. The department head replied, "Yes, only on an 'occasional' basis."

About two months later both Robin and another employee were reported for violating the dress code set by the department head by wearing blue jeans. As a result, Robin and some other employees wanted a specific explanation of the word "occasional." The response they received was that all employees should "use their own judgment" as to the frequency of wearing blue jeans. Clearly, there was no reason to leave such a policy to personal judgment when they could have been specific about it.

Soon the issue of creating such deliberate ambiguity came out in the open. The reason was that the human resources unit of the corporation was the only department with the authority to make organizational decisions on the dress code. With this understanding, on one hand, the department head did not want to see his employees being so casual. On the other hand, he did not have the authority to formulate or enforce such a policy.

There are other motives for creating ambiguity or misunderstanding, some of which are reviewed below.

Playing Neutral In one of the well-known drug manufacturing firms there is a constant friction between the technology department and the quality control department: The technology department is eager to come up with new products and send them through the production department in order to market them before competitors do. This relatively fast-paced process may result in an approximate one-percent quality defect rate in the marketed products. The quality control department, on the other hand, insists on a zero defect rate. When this matter came to the attention of the CEO of the corporation, his intention was to maintain ambiguity. The CEO has extensive sales and marketing experience, and favors fast-paced production. This way, not only will the drug company become a pioneer for providing a given product to the market, ultimately it will also make the stockholders jubilant. The other side of the matter is that anything less than a zero percent defect rate is a risk with regard to the health of the patients, and a serious threat to the reputation of the company.

Additionally, if the CEO insists on maintaining a zero defect rate, it would ultimately disenchant the technology and production departments. Should he be willing to compromise with a lower level of quality, it would disappoint the quality control department as well. Therefore, brushing off the matter and maintaining some sort of ambiguity was a selected alternative for the CEO.

Don't Have Any Appetite In most Western countries, when acquaintances or extended families go to a restaurant, it is common that there will be separate checks for each party in the group. In some other countries, the check usually goes to the older person, unless otherwise specified to the server.

On one occasion, about five individuals went to a restaurant. Among them was a clever man with a fatherly look and graying hair who knew that the check would probably come to him, something that he did not want to happen. Therefore, while in the presence of the waiter, who was ready to take the orders, in a casual and subtle way the man declared, "I don't know why I have really no appetite at all." This was a way to imply that he should not pick up the tab. One of the individuals at the table said, "We don't want you to be hungry, why don't you have something light, at least!" The man responded, "Well, since you insist I will."

At the end, when the server brought the bill, he didn't know to whom to give it? The formation of this ambiguity by the clever man actually did work for him, and someone else had to pick up the tab.

As we shall see, most misunderstandings are not deliberate because a word or a sentence may mean different things to one individual or another.

Written Information Have you come across reading about benefits that you are entitled to with your heath insurance coverage and you found it hard to understand? A manager of a human resource department of an accounting firm shared the following with me. He pointed out that some health insurance companies intentionally write down the benefits that are provided by them in a rather confusing way. The purpose is for the insurance holder to be unaware of all the benefits. He also added that he has come across some insurance claim applications with intentional complications to discourage the submission of a claim. For example, requesting many dates of events that would be difficult to remember.

These insurance forms are similar to many credit card contract agreements. These agreements used to be limited to one or two pages; their contents were straightforward, easy to read and understand. Nowadays, all too often, these contracts are expanded to several pages, so that a reader may become overwhelmed by reading them. As a result, a lawyer's assistant may be needed to interpret them. What do you think are the reasons for these lengthy and complicated contracts?

Final Notes

In this chapter we reviewed the many faces of misunderstandings within and between various cultural settings. Some ambiguities were crafted, and others were unintentional. We explained and demonstrated the simplicity of creating inadvertent misunderstanding with its wide range of outcomes. An understanding of the communication process and its dynamics is an effective approach in dealing with many communication breakdowns.

ENDNOTES

1. David A. Ricks, *Blunders in International Business* (Malden, MA: Blackwell, 1993).

2. Ed Magnuson "Can Planes Just Run Out of Gas?," *Time,* February 12, 1990, p. 24; James T. McKenna, "CVR Shows Avianca Crew Knew Fuel Was Too Low," *Aviation Week and & Space Technology,* April 2, 1990. pp. 52-3.

3. "Air Travel: How Safe?," *Time,* April 11, 1977. pp.22-26; "KLM Pilot on Collision Reportedly Didn't Hear Controller's 'Stand By'," *The New York Times,* April 9, 1977. p.2.

4. "Minister De Transportes," Joint Report K.L.M.-P.A.A. 12.7. 1978, *Colision Aeronves Boeing 747 PH-BUF DE K.L.M. Y Boeing 747 N 736 PA de Pan Am En Los Rodeos (Tenerife),* EL 27 De Marzo De 1.977., 12.7.1978.

5. Gerald M. Golghaber, *Organizational Communication,* 3rd. ed. (Dubuque, IW: Wm. C. Brown, 1983), p.124.

6. John W. Newstrom and Keith Davis, *Organizational Behavior: Human Behavior Work,* 9th ed. (New York: McGraw Hill, 1993), p.91.

RECOMMENDED READING

Andrew J. DuBrin. *Human Relations: A Job Oriented Approach.* Englewood Cliffs, NJ: Prentice Hall, 1992.

Deborah Tannen. *That's Not What I Meant!* New York: Ballantine Books, 1986.

Iris Varner and Linda Beamer. *Intercultural Communication in the Global Workplace.* Boston: McGraw Hill/Irwin, 2005.

Keith Davis. *Popular American Colloquialisms: Their Meaning and Origin.* Tempe, AZ: Keith Davis, 1991.

CHAPTER FOUR

MANAGEMENT AND COMMUNICATION IN COMPLEX ORGANIZATIONS

Communication in organizations is becoming more complex, leaving more room for ambiguities. For example, in traditional organizations, purchasing personnel had to communicate with one superior to give reports or receive purchasing instructions. Nowadays, such a buyer typically needs to communicate with the budgeting department to determine the allowed maximum purchasing price. Additionally, the buyer has to communicate with the department for which equipment is going to be purchased for information about specifications and performance, as well as with the immediate superior in the purchasing department.

The aim of this chapter is to discuss several concerns of communication that hamper overall organizational effectiveness. We begin with the employee interview process.

Joanne is a supervisory administrator in the human resources department of a midsized health care clinic in Maryland. One of her functions is conducting yearly performance reviews of the personnel. Joanne has authority to increase an employee's salary up to five percent per year, depending on the level of displayed performance.

Linda is among one of the highest performing nurses in the clinic. She also goes out of her way to help patients, physicians, and other nurses in the clinic.

It is that time of the year that Linda's performance is going to be reviewed by Joanne. In the performance appraisal, nothing is falling short in the overall quality of work Linda has delivered. As always, she has wonderful interpersonal skills with everyone, superior knowledge, and more time in the clinic as normally expected of nurses. Using these considerations, Joanne gladly offers the maximum raise of five percent on her salary.

From Linda's perspective, this offer is not sufficient vis-à-vis her level of performance. She wants a raise of at least eight percent. Despite being in agreement with Linda's view, Joanne cannot offer any more than a five-percent increase in her yearly salary.

Disenchanted, Linda decides to take her case, to John, who is Joanne's immediate superior. It does not take too much effort to convince John to agree to a raise of eight percent.

Possible outcomes of this occurrence could be as follows:

1. Ambiguity is created for Joanne. John, on several occasions, has emphasized the importance of following the rules and policies of the

organization. Yet he himself ignores them. John's instructions tend not to be taken seriously by Joanne.

2. Although Linda is happy because she received what she requested, she is rather confused and even suspicious of Joanne's sincerity. In the performance review, Joanne had acknowledged Linda's superior work, and yet she did not seem to care enough to give her an eight-percent raise in salary.

3. It was a lesson for others who witnessed Linda's actions: if you complain enough, you can get what you want in this department.

Situations like this are not uncommon. Incidents of ambiguities and misunderstandings occur more than seldom in many aspects of organizations, some of which can be reviewed here.

Employment: Interview and Evaluation

The employment interview is one of the major steps in the hiring process, determining whether the job description and specifications are congruent. This step is a congruency between the job description and the job specifications.[1] This step is also an opportunity for the interviewee to learn more about the organization while deciding to work for it. Some of the conditions that impede effective interviews are as follows.

Halo Effect This term can be defined as a snapshot of someone's appearance, behavior, verbal communication skills, or knowledge as a basis for developing a generalization about that individual.

In an employment interview session, a job seeker's first few answers may be grounds for the interviewer to draw a positive picture of the job seeker. Subsequently, the interviewer may process further responses from that individual in a more favorable way.

Projection This is when someone believes having similar values and attributes of others. For example, someone who has a habit of exaggerating when describing an event to make it more exciting may assume that others have the same habit. In other words, when such an individual listens to an interesting event, he may feel that it has been inflated.

Projection can be unfair in many situations, including hiring practices. Mr. F., an interviewer for a furniture manufacturing company, is a rather introverted and unsociable individual. He attempts to display a sociable and friendly façade only when the situation requires it. Mr. F. interviews a job seeker who is well mannered and friendly, but may assume that his manner and friendliness are superficial, in order to paint a different picture of himself. As a result, Mr. F. may offer the position to a less qualified individual.

Perception Perception is commonly known as contrast effect, which can affect one's initial views. Suppose the chair of an academic department is interviewing several candidates for a full-time teaching position. Suppose also that the first few candidates are able to impress the chair with their teaching experience and other academic qualifications. The next candidate, Professor H., has his own set of qualifications, but they are not quite as impressive as the others. On a comparative basis, the chair may perceive him to be less qualified than he really is.

In an opposite scenario, if the chair has interviewed a few candidates who barely possess the minimum required qualifications. Professor H.'s qualifications then would look considerably better.

The chairperson may develop a less favorable perception of Professor H. in the first situation and a more favorable one in the second. Similar qualifications could be perceived differently by the same individual.

Groupthink Generally speaking, conformity is important to a group maintenance and decision-making process. However, an emphasis on conformity while overlooking the purpose of group formation leads to what is known as groupthink, which potentially results in unwanted consequences.[2]

Recently, one of the hospitals on the East Coast announced several position openings for well-qualified psychiatrists. The hospital offered competitive salaries and a series of attractive benefits. Of many applicants, only a few were selected for interviews based on the qualifications and credentials shown on their submitted resumes. Each candidate was interviewed by a panel of interviewers, and finally a few psychiatrists were selected for the positions.

After the panel interviews with each candidate, the interviewers had a meeting to discuss their views on each candidate. One of the interviewers was apprehensive about hiring Mr. P., who was one of the candidates. The interviewer refrained from discussing his concern about Mr. P. during the meeting, and Mr. P. eventually was hired for the psychiatric section of the hospital. A few months later, it was found that almost all of the submitted credentials and documents were falsified. Subsequently, he was dismissed from the position.

The question is, why did the interviewer who was apprehensive about hiring Mr. P. not bring the matter into the open during the meeting for the selection process? It was because the interviewer happened to be the youngest and the least experienced member of the panel. He felt insecure about disagreeing with the other interviewers who had predominately positive impressions of Mr. P.

This is a typical case of groupthink. It is essential to create an environment that encourages all group members to speak openly, regardless of their level of experience or position.

Focusing on Results All too often, assessment of performance is based solely on the outcome, which by itself creates misunderstanding regarding employee performance. The way in which a job has been done must be taken into consideration for performance evaluation. The following experience illustrates that.

In most large furniture stores, it is typical that each sales associate takes a turn helping the incoming customers, whereby each associate should have equal chance to make a sale and earn the sale's commission. In this process, there are some sales associates who try to talk to more than one customer at a time without considering the other associates' turns to approach customers. Many of these sales associates also tend to be overly assertive with the customer in trying to make a sale. Therefore, these sales associates could affect the mood of other associates on the floor. Also, a customer may purchase an item, but may never want to come back to that store, which ultimately would be a loss to the store.

Having that illustration in mind, we see that a sales person may achieve the highest sales performance using this behavior, but at a cost of being unfair to other sales associates and driving away many customers. Performance appraisal should not only account for a given result, but also for the employee's mean of achieving that result.

Playing Politics

More than seldom, playing politics occurs between people in most organizations. It happens between managers and workers. The manager says, "You should have your promotion very soon," while knowing such possibility is very minimal. The manager's misleading comment is intended to keep the worker on the job longer because of his high performance. Many workers also come up with comments that are not straightforward. I know of an administrative assistant who used to have migraines frequently, especially every time she found herself in an overloaded work situation. As a result, the work was directed to others for completion. Later, because of her educational background and her know-how in a specific area, she was promoted to another position that she enjoyed. Since then, her migraines seemed to be cured.

Playing politics also happens with or by people outside of an organization. Mr. B. was the owner of an educational institution with about three hundred employees. Occasionally, friends or acquaintances would go to him seeking a position. One of his acquaintances, Ms. J., contacted him for a position. For the purpose of saving face, Mr. B. assured her that he would send a strong recommendation to the pertinent department.

Indeed, Mr. B. contacted the department head about Ms. J., but stated that he did not want her to be part of the organization. Ms. J. did not know why she was not hired, despite the recommendation by the president of the organization. The point here is that Mr. B. was giving positive responses to maintain good relationships with people he knew outside of his organization, but not all of them got what they wanted, meaning a position in Mr. B's establishment.

Interacting with Employees: A Matter of Inconsistency

In this section I will refer to two areas of concern as related to superiors and employees. First, I will discuss the deliberate formation of ambiguity and inconsistency of behavior as a seemingly effective approach to productivity. Second, I will discuss inconsistency in providing feedback to employees.

Creative Ambiguity Some years ago I was engaged in consulting for an accounting firm. I noticed that one of the managerial practices of the firm was to hire graduate students from reputable universities for entry level accounting positions. This way, the new entrants had the opportunity to gain first-hand experience while the accounting firm was able to pay them a lower salary than experienced accountants.

One of the departmental managers, Mr. D., was working with about twelve of these new accountants. He was more demanding of his employees than most managers in the firm. Mr. D. was sometimes quite sociable, friendly, and helpful, and other times he chose to be quite the opposite. Because of the noticeable variation in his behavior, it was difficult to communicate with him.

One summer morning, I was in my temporary office when one of the new accountants wanted to speak with me in private. She hesitantly asked me if she had done something wrong. Surprised by her question, I replied, "No, nothing that I know of." On the verge of tears, she said that this morning she had seen Mr. D. in the hallway, waved at him, and said good morning. She saw no expression on his face, as if she were not there. He then looked down while passing her. I told her that she should not take this personally, as he had probably had a bad day. Soon after this incident, another similar situation occurred with another new accountant.

In an informal gathering, my curiosity had encouraged me to ask Mr. D. about his change of behavior in the workplace. He pointed out that sometimes creating a state of ambiguity motivates employees to be "on their toes." "If they cannot read my mind, then they prefer to do their best," he said.

Unsuccessfully, I voiced my view that ambiguity is worrisome, which decreases the efficiency and effectiveness of their work. Also, as a matter of fairness, management should form a suitable working environment for employees. Gradually,

through interaction with Mr. D., the new accountants came to recognize the motive for his behavior.

Feedback There are some managers whose
deep concern for task accomplishment and meeting
deadlines takes priority over good relations with
employees. On the other hand, some are so
excessively concerned with keeping employees
happy, that they overlook their tasks and responsi-
bilities.

Eric was working for over a year in the production
line of a pharmaceutical company. Not only was his
performance below average, but he often came to
work late. And he wanted to chat with other
employees while working. All of these factors lend
themselves to some type of bottleneck situation in
the work process. Unexpectedly, his team leader,
John, was overly concerned with keeping everyone
happy and did not exhibit sufficient concern about
job accomplishment. Eric received a favorable
performance assessment, but John did not provide
Eric with an objective and impartial feedback
regarding his lateness and wasting time while at
work.

Later on, the company announced a job opening,
which would have been a promotion for Eric.
Enthusiastically, Eric applied for the position. Later,
he was notified that he was not among those who
were selected for an interview. There was a
misunderstanding concerning Eric: considering that
he had all the qualifications for the position, and he
received consistently positive feedback for his job
performance, why was he not even considered for the
initial interview? The issue was later routed to upper
management for review.

Constructive feedback should be a part of downward communication. It is important to provide employees with honest and impartial comments concerning their performance and conduct. Misleading feedback could cause confusion and disappointment.

Variation of Personality in the Workplace

Individuals' personalities fall between two broad categories, personality A and personality B. Each category has its own distinct set of characteristics. For example, those with personality A tend to be in a rush and, trying to perform more than one task concurrently. They are very goal oriented with an urgency to finish work way before its deadline; they are competitive and prefer hard work over leisure. On the other hand, people with personality B are more laid back and less competitive and appreciate relaxation.

An individual with strong personality A working with a person with personality B could create disagreements and misunderstandings. The following is a scenario of such a situation.

In the admission department of a large university, John recently was hired as the director of that department. The new director had an assistant, Joanne, who had been working in the same position for several years.

The director was not very efficient in his work vis-à-vis his highly demanding tasks. Additionally, the director with an obvious personality A wanted to do even more than was required and met all the deadlines beforehand. On the other hand, his assistant was very efficient with a laid back approach.

Each day, the director gave Joanne a number of tasks to perform and kept wasting his time and Joann's time by sending multiple e-mails for updates about the work progress.

Soon an increasing level of frustrations and misunderstandings was noticed. John was thinking that Joanne deliberately was delaying the work in a way that the new director would look "bad" in front of his superior, which was not the case. In the meantime, the assistant was thinking that John was trying to replace her by deliberately micromanaging her, which was not the case either because for one thing, John who was new on the job did not want to "rock the boat" as that could have been a barrier to his future promotional opportunities. Additionally, John knew that his attempt to replace Joanne was improbable, as she proved to be a capable assistant working for many years with the previous directors.

Customer Satisfaction

It was midmorning one summer when I came home with my newly purchased desktop computer. I anxiously opened the package, read the owner's manual, and started its setup. On the panel of the computer I saw an 800 number for technical support, available 24/7. Seeing this made me feel comfortable about my purchase. Should I have any difficulty, someone would be there to help me out. During the process, I came up with a technical question. That morning, unsuccessfully, I tried a few times to speak with someone. Each time I called, I waited about fifteen minutes before hanging up the phone. Each time, there was a recording repeatedly apologizing for the inconvenience, and assuring that someone would be with me shortly. I noticed a discrepancy between what I saw on the panel of the computer for technical support and what I was experiencing.

Early that afternoon I called again, but this time I was determined to wait as long as it would take to speak with someone for my technical question. I waited for about half an hour, listening to the same annoying repeated message. While waiting and holding the portable phone handset, I went to sleep in my rocking chair. It was over an hour later that I heard a voice saying "Hello? Hello?" I woke up, and at first I did not know who was calling me; I realized it was the technician. I said, "Please don't hang up," then I asked my question. But he could not really help me because he was new on the job, and no other technician was available to come to the phone. With considerable disappointment, the next day I returned the computer to the store, exchanging it for another brand. After this experience I had no reason to believe that the company would be in business for long. About six months later, they went out of business.

Here is another scenario related to the issue of customer satisfaction. In a gathering, a bank teller shared this. She mentioned that in the branch where she works, there are not enough tellers to effectively help customers. As a result, the branch manager receives more than a few complaints about the long wait. This is how it happens. While waiting on a customer in the bank, she also needs to help the drive-through customers. Meanwhile, a supervisor comes to her with a question about an account. In the midst of all this, another customer calls, saying that she just received her statement, which shows a charge that cannot be accounted for. She said that while the customer is waiting on the line she brings the matter to the head teller, but she is quite busy helping others. She is told to get the customer's phone number for a later callback. For the customer, who is upset and worried about the possibility of insufficient funds for writing checks, the word "later" is unacceptable. Understanding the customer's frustration, the teller goes to see the branch manager, but he is in a teleconference and cannot be interrupted. When she returns to the phone, the customer has already hung up. Soon after, the customer closed her account and wrote a letter of complaint to the corporate office.

It seems quite puzzling that a company would choose a managerial approach that leads to customers' as well as employees' dissatisfaction, taking into account that such an approach would create customer dissatisfaction and deepen employee turnover, both of which curtail a company's success and prosperity.

Moreover, it is puzzling that many corporations spend millions of dollars in their promotional activities, particularly advertising, to bring in new customers while they pay almost no attention to keeping them.

Caring about Customers In a graduate marketing course, a session was devoted to open discussions on the topic of customer satisfaction and loyalty. Names such as SAS, which is the world's largest privately owned software establishment, Nordstrom, American Express, LL Bean, Ritz Carlton, and Xerox were among so many other companies with excellent customer service reputations that were mentioned. But there are many others that provide substandard services to their customers. One of the students, who was working as a technician in a large communication company, shared the following experience.

Answering the phone and speaking to customers with technical questions is her line of work. She asserted that, strangely enough, they were instructed **not** to pick up the phone promptly. The reason is to find out the average waiting threshold of their customers; in other words, how long it takes for a customer to become impatient and hang up the phone. This way the company can keep only the minimum number of technical representatives needed to keep their customers happy. The company's misunderstanding about this approach is that it may lead to short-term profitability by paying less in salaries, but in a competitive environment, it will threaten organizational growth and prosperity.

Thomas Jones and W. Earl Sasser, Jr. emphasized the importance of complete customer satisfaction. They reported that a comprehensive study conducted by Xerox Corporation revealed that "Its totally satisfied customers were six times more likely to repurchase Xerox products over the next 18 months than its satisfied customers. The implications were profound: merely satisfying customers who have the freedom to make choices is not enough to keep them loyal." [3]

Why Are Companies Falling Short in Customer Satisfaction? All of us probably have had a taste of receiving a substandard service in one way or another. There could be an array of possible reasons for these experiences, such as employee work overload, lack of motivation, or lack of accountability. However, in this section we can look at the lack of (adequate) commitment and loyalty on a reciprocal basis between employers and employees that can ultimately spill over to customer dissatisfaction.

There has been case after case in which an experienced employee was replaced by a younger individual for the sake of paying a lower salary. Many employees also leave their present jobs for even a slight salary increase elsewhere, overlooking years of built relationships.

With this condition of high employee turnover, an upper manager can anticipate leaving his present firm within the next few years. This upper manager, therefore, can select between one of the two following alternatives. The first is to purchase better equipment as needed, as well as provide various training programs, both technical and interpersonal for employees. Of course, such an approach initially decreases organizational performance because employees will be spending time learning and training instead of being on the job to do their usual work. Moreover, there will be costs for training and purchasing advanced equipment. The end result is that for the first few years, the costs of operation will be higher with a lower production level. Such results may not be an addition to the credentials of that manager when he leaves that organization for another position. The second alternative would be to push sales and cut costs as much as possible. Therefore, quality of both services and products are compromised, which ultimately affects customer satisfaction and organizational competitiveness.

Considering that a committed employee is the backbone of quality products and consumer satisfaction, I propose the following five interrelated steps: "the Five Cs Approach to Organizational

Relationships." It is evident that the applicability and practicality of these approaches may vary significantly from one organization to another:

1. **Connectivity** At this starting point, to bring about a better understanding of the organization's mission to its employees is highly essential. The management should disseminate the purpose of the organization and its standing toward its "stakeholders," which would allow employees to work toward a common organizational goal.

2. **Communication** Through a periodic, random sampling process, management can communicate with employees. This could pave the way to open and sincere communication to uncover their fair and realistic expectation of the organizational management, such as job security, a variable pay plan, educational subsidies, or flexible benefit plans. The organizational expectation should be spelled out as well. Would they be paying more attention to quality products, teamwork, or coming forward with any pertinent problems or recommendations? As a result, the organization could formulate a realistic action plan that meets reciprocal expectations.

3. **Coaching** The management of an organization should have the opportunity to seek assistance from outside consulting experts to assess the efficiency and effectiveness of its planning and its implementation, and to receive insights as needed.

4. **Cooperation** This phase denotes a give-and-take type of effort. The management commits itself to positive employee motivation, while the employees are engaged in doing what they

are supposed to do for the organization. The cooperation from one side tends to diminish with a lack of cooperation from the other side. Continuous cooperation will set the stage for the next phase.

5. **Commitment** Such a condition represents some sort of partnership between the two parties. Each side genuinely tries to do good work for the benefit of the other party, for mutual benefit. The organization recognizes that its customer satisfaction and financial prosperity is embedded in employee satisfaction. Equally, the employee will be able to find a direct relationship between his commitment to his work and personal satisfaction.

Richard Florida and Jim Goodnight in *Harvard Business Review* commented that the relationship between employee satisfaction and prosperity can be noted in SAS Institute, a software company in North Carolina. It is the largest privately owned company of its kind in the world. A major focus of the company is its employee satisfaction, and SAS is enjoying tremendous financial success.[4]

Management Effectiveness

As we are coming to the closing of this chapter, let me explore some of the aspects of managerial effectiveness. It is an oversimplification to assume that because one style of management is effective in one setting, then it should be effective in all situations. With this consideration, the following major components of effective management will be taken into account. (See Exhibit 4.1).

1) Our own preferred style of management: Comfort Zone

2) Determinant factors within organizations: Microenvironment

3) Determinant factors outside of organizations: Macroenvironment.

Comfort Zone The managerial style falls into three broad categories. First is the laissez-faire, approach by which managers allow employees to make decisions. They call upon their manager as necessary. Second is the democratic approach where managerial decisions are made through collaboration with employees. Third is the autocratic, where emphasis is on one-way communication. Managers make the decisions and announce them to the employees for implementation.

The preferred style of management is based on the way that makes managers feel more comfortable. This may very well be because of the way they were treated as employees by their superiors. For example, one who has been working for an authoritarian manager could acquire the same style if that individual were to become a manager.

From the employee's perspective, there is a variation in desired managerial styles. "Employees in some cultures want their superiors to be ... decisive and authoritarian. Latin American employees, for example, may feel uncomfortable with a boss who delegates too much authority to them. In other cultures, such as Scandinavian, employees want their managers to emphasize a participative, problem-solving approach".[5]

Microenvironment Within an organization, there are at least four determinants that may influence managerial styles. The first has to do with the urgency to accomplish tasks. For example, when a fire department is notified of a "call" in a nearby building, there is no time for participative decision making. The person in charge takes a course of action and announces it. The second determinant is organizational culture. In many societies, employees of an organization perceive an effective manager as the one with all the necessary knowledge and determination to make decisions. This is why they are paid and respected or, as is commonly referred to, this is why they are making the "big bucks." With this concept, managers with laissez-faire or participative approaches may not be suitable. The third is the level of knowledge and expertise of employees. Employees who have acquired the desired know-how create a more suitable environment for participative decisions. Through this, managers are able to utilize their input and further ameliorate both the morale of the employees and the quality of their products. The fourth determinant concerns the importance of a quality product. In an organization that emphasizes quality improvement on a continual basis, participative management seems to be most appropriate. Vertical communication should be intact. Managers instruct, guide, motivate, assign tasks, and provide feedback (downward communication). Employees ask questions, and provide superiors with unfiltered reports for both progress and problems, and are able to share ideas and suggestions with their manager (upward communication). Open, two-way communication is a major component of participative managerial style.

Macroenvironment In addition to the comfort zone of managers and the determinants of the organizational environment, there is another area of concern: macroenvironment. The first concern is the attitude of a society toward the pace of work. In many societies, hard work is a virtue. Someone once said that in Tokyo, it is uncommon for an individual to be walking in a residential area rather than being at work. However, in many other cultural settings, less work and more socialization and enjoyment of life are common trends. Second is the issue of planning. In probably every textbook on management published in the United States, there is a chapter devoted to the process, importance, and range of planning. However, not every society perceives planning to be highly crucial. This is because one may not be able to look into the future. In addition, the current era represents tremendous economic, technological, and political changes and unpredictability. The third concern is in regard to the degree of collaboration in the workplace. In some cultures there is a minimal amount of teamwork. On the other hand, in many other cultural settings, such as those in most Asian countries, teamwork is reinforced because it creates synergy toward task accomplishments.

The observation of how people interact in social and business settings in a given society may provide us with some fair assessments of how people interact and communicate in respective organizations. The impact of the macroenvironment on corporate management is noteworthy. One of the multibillion dollar European investment companies has launched an extensive management training program for one of its overseas subsidiaries. The overall purpose of that training was to foster collaboration and participative decision making at supervisory and midmanagement levels. The training programs were conducted without taking into account the external setting. The determinants of the macroenvironment in which the subsidiary was located were not in harmony with the intended managerial training programs. As a result, what had been learned in the training programs would soon evaporate. As another example, Swiss Air unsuccessfully attempted to improve efficiency, teamwork, and customer service in several branches around the globe.

Considering the reinforcement of the external setting, such training programs are not always a success. A higher level of effectiveness in training may be achieved by addressing these considerations. Managers, particularly those with international missions, should recognize the importance of assessing their managerial comfort zones as well as the determinants of the microenvironment and macroenvironment. Such assessment is helped by an open, impartial, and receptive mind. This is essential to selecting an appropriate managerial style.

EXHIBIT 4.1

DETERMINANTS OF MANAGERIAL EFFECTIVENESS

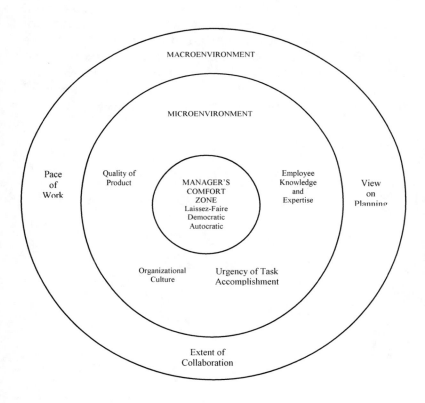

Final Notes

We have examined many pitfalls associated with hiring employees. We have also examined an understanding of the role of employees in customer satisfaction, which is essential in a competitive market. Another issue in complex organizations is with regard to the management itself. As described, each organization has its own norms and culture. Effective leadership is rooted in such understanding and the ability to adapt an approach conducive to overall organizational effectiveness.

ENDNOTES

1. "Job description" can be defined as the information that explains activities, duties, authorities, and responsibility attached to the job, as well as working conditions and equipment. "Job specification" specifies minimum qualifications required of the individual for the job, which includes both academic background and work experience.

2. Pamela A. Angel, *Business Communication Design: Creativity, Strategies, and Solutions,* 2nd ed. (New York: McGraw Hill/Irwin, 2007), p. 393.

3. Thomas O. Jones and W. Earl Sasser, Jr., "Why Satisfied Customers Defect," *Harvard Business Review* (November-December 1995): pp. 88-99, quote in p. 91.

4. Richard Florida and Jim Goodnight, "Managing for Creativity," *Harvard Business Review* (Jul-Aug 2005): pp.125-131.

5. John R. Schermerhorn, Jr., James G. Hunt, and Richard N Osborn, *Managing Organizational Behavior,* 4th ed. (New York: John Wiley & Sons, 1991), p. 87.

RECOMMENDED READING

Donald G. Mosley, Paul H. Pietri, and Leon c. Megginson. *Management: Leadership in Action.* New York: HarperCollins College Publishers, 1996.

Gary Dressler. *Human Resource Management.* Upper Saddle River, NJ: Pearson Prentice Hall. 2005.

Gareth R. Jones and Jennifer M. George. *Contemporary Management*. New York: McGraw Hill/Irwin, 2008.

Richard M. Hodgetts and Fred Luthans. *International Management*. New York: McGraw Hill, 1997.

Wayne D. Hoyer and Deborah J. MacInnis. *Consumer Behavior*. Boston: Houghton Mifflin Company, 2007.

CHAPTER FIVE

MARKETING AMBIGUITY

The field of marketing is not immune to the intentional and well-planned formation of ambiguity. In our discussion, a range of examples of promotional strategies and other marketing activities will be given, particularly from international perspectives. To proceed, let us briefly review the evolution of marketing in the United States, as it will provide a base for our analysis. (See Exhibit 5.1)

An Overview of Marketing Evolution in the United States

The Embryonic Stage Toward the later part of the 1850s, the gap between the supply of and the demand for goods and services was significant. In other words, the ability and willingness to produce was much smaller than the need and ability to purchase. The proverb "necessity is the mother of invention" applies here because this gap led the way to the formation of assembly lines and mass production as well as the invention and production of many items, including the dishwasher, the elevator, the telephone, the light bulb, and the television, to name a few. Therefore, the concentration was on production to meet the everincreasing demand.

This condition created a sellers' market. Customers could not be too choosy or demanding. If one customer, for example, did not like the color of a pair of shoes that she wanted to buy, surely there was another customer who wanted to buy that item. Furthermore, the concept of market segmentation and target marketing was not a concern for the marketer. There was a demand for virtually every product.

The Growth Stage In the 1920s, there was a continuous growing trend of assembly lines, mechanical and technical improvements, and improved efficiency in the production process. As a result, there was more availability of goods and services, which lessened the dependency of buyers on a single supplier. Producers and suppliers recognized the importance of bringing more variety of colors, sizes, packaging, functionality, and styles as a means to attract customers.

The Expansive Stage The advancement of technology, assembly lines, and mass production, took the availability of products to a new high. Consequently, in the 1950s there was no notable gap between the supply of and the demand for goods and services. Rather, the abundance of products created many choices for the buyers. As a result, a gradual change from a "sellers' market" to a "buyers' market" began.

It was understood that simply improving the quality of a product was not sufficient to create a positive edge against the competition. It was time for the sellers to learn about the techniques of selling strategies for successful marketing endeavors. Some of them are as follows:

- Do not ask customers if they want to buy an item. Assume that they want to buy it. So, give them a choice: ask them which color are they interested in. Green or blue?

- Try to talk about the price at the end of your presentation; once you capture their interest, and then give them the price.

- Through listening and observation, find out who is the ultimate decision maker. If for example, a married couple is looking for bedroom furniture to buy, pay attention to the person who seems to be the decision maker.

- Do not ask for a signature, but ask for an autograph. The word signature might scare most buyers.

- In some cases, act as if this is the last item with the color and size that the customer wants. How lucky!

The Presaturation Stage In this stage, we see a new gap between supply and demand. This time, the supply arrow has gained a positive edge over the arrow of the demand. It is a continuous trend before our eyes: the dramatic expansion of technology, modernization, and innovation in so many fields such as transportation, energy, health, agriculture, and communication. In addition to this trend, beginning in the early 1970s, we have seen a monumental amount of product importation into the United States.

When you enter into your neighborhood drug store to buy shampoo, you will see so many choices that it may become difficult to choose one among them. For example, there are shampoos for newborn babies, for those with colored hair, and for those with dandruff. There are shampoos for thin, oily, dry, curly, or soft hair. There are organic shampoos, and shampoos with a variety of scents. The list will go on.

In addition to the drastic increase in productivity and imported products, both durable and nondurable, there was another factor that diminished the vigor of selling techniques. Customers were continually becoming more informed about products that they wanted to buy, thanks to the easy availability of data, such as the fair-market value of a given used car. Marketers therefore had to rely on extensive marketing research and product development to find their target market and provide it with the exact goods and services those customers wanted to purchase.

The Saturation Stage A saturated market with so many suppliers has provided a new layer of challenge for sellers. Offering exactly what the customer wants does not necessarily mean that a supplier retains and maintains its competitive edge. Many suppliers are now trying to find ways to give their customers something beyond their expectations to earn their loyalty.

Exhibit 5.1

A Conceptual Gap between the Supply of and the Demand for Goods and Services During the Evolution of Marketing in the United States:

STAGES OF MARKETING DEVELOPMENT

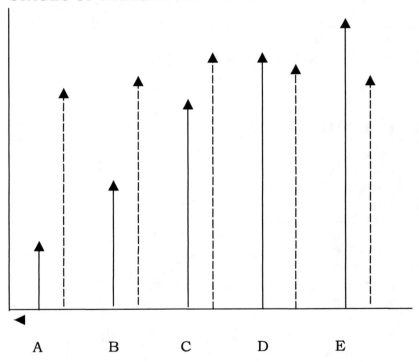

A   B   C   D   E

The Stages:
A Embryonic   B Growth
C Expansive   D Presaturation
E Saturation

Supply   Demand
⟶   -----▶

Nordstrom is one of the most successful upscale clothing department stores in the United States. The chain has an unflinching commitment to customer's satisfaction. I have heard about a customer experience with the store. In the 1970s, a customer walked into a Nordstrom department store to return a pair of tires for a refund. The associate saw the price tag on the tires, and accordingly refunded the customer for the tires. Apparently, the location used to be a tire store, where the customer had purchased the tires. He simply wanted to return them to the same location where he bought them.

Encountering the Unexpected

Not all marketers are committed to customer loyalty and satisfaction. Many marketers select different approaches to stay competitive. Most of us have come across such marketing techniques that were not expected and have formed some sort of misunderstanding. They could have been intentional or coincidental, pertinent to pricing or quantity of products, or promotional strategies, a few of which will be examined.

No Matter What, I Am the Winner

While living in Colorado, one day as usual; I opened my mailbox for incoming letters. On top of the other mail, I saw an envelope with bold letters stating that it was urgent and I must open it immediately, which I did. There was good news! I was the winner of an expensive new automobile or an eight-carat genuine diamond. To claim my prize I needed to drive to Brackenridge, Colorado, and participate in a sales presentation to buy land or a condominium.

It seemed too good to be true. In other words, I knew there had to be a catch but did not know what. Out of curiosity, my family and I drove to the designated location and participated in the sales seminar. There was a sales team that tried in many ways to close a sale, which created a very unpleasant experience. At the end, when we claimed our prize, we were told that we did not win the automobile, but the diamond ring. But again there was a catch, as I initially expected. Can you guess what it was? Was the diamond genuine? Yes. Was it of less total weight than specified? No. Was it of poor quality? Not necessarily. The fact was that the ring was composed of enormous particles of diamonds that were glued together. Apparently, these tiny pieces were gathered during the shaping and cutting process of the genuine diamonds. That was our prize! Something with no appeal and no value, which was immediately placed in a trash can.

Misleading Volume There was an advertisement on television showing a man with a fit body walking in the woods while eating crunchy cereal. He was placing his thumb and forefinger in a full box of cereal, grabbing some, and putting it in his mouth. This advertisement stayed in my mind as I related health and nature to eating cereals. In another advertisement, there was a happy family at a breakfast table, having their cereal with milk. One morning I arranged a table similar to the one I saw in the advertisement and enthusiastically headed to my neighborhood grocery store to buy a box of cereal. I could not find what I saw on television but bought another that looked appealing. While at the table, I opened the box and wanted to eat some of it before pouring it into a bowl. I put my hand in the box to grab some and unexpectedly could not find any cereal. I looked for cereal even deeper, but still I could not find any. Curiously, I looked in the box and noticed that almost half of it was empty.

On my next visit to the store, I spoke with one of the employees about the box of cereal. He replied that almost all of them are that way, which I had a difficult time believing. Randomly, I purchased another box of cereal, mainly to satisfy my curiosity. The next day I opened the box for my breakfast, and I realized that the employee was right—a significant portion of the box was again empty. On the cover, in very small type, there was an 800 number for customer relations. After a long wait, someone came on the line and asked many questions, such as my name, street address, and where I purchased the cereal. Needless to say, such data can be used as invaluable marketing data. I expressed my concern to the representative about the size of these boxes in relation to the volume of cereal inside. She commented that the boxes are actually full when they leave the plant. They go through a settling process during transportation before customers purchase them. I then asked her if, as a customer, she would like buying a can of soup that was about 40 percent empty. I also proposed, to minimize any misunderstanding, that they do the settling before the packages leave the plant. She replied that it was a very good point. She would share that with management and someone would get back me. To this date, no one from that cereal company has returned my call.

In many vending machines, you will see a pack of candies or pretzels that look full, as many of them are shown through a clear window. Once you put money in the machine to purchase them, you will soon find that about half of the bag is empty. This is because the contents of the bag are strategically placed. Notice that if you turned upside-down, it would look completely empty through that clear window.

Some years ago, some of my friends and I went to a restaurant. There, I saw large glasses of drinks brought to the tables, which was quite enticing. When the server was taking the orders, I asked for a soft drink with my dinner. A few minutes later, a large glassful of soda sat on our table. However, it was much less than it initially appeared. The reason was the unusual thickness of the glass.

Misleading Pricing There was a program on television that showed how some department stores claim that their products storewide were on sale for 20 to 50 percent off, which was a misrepresentation. These stores set inflationary prices on their merchandise prior to sales. Afterward, customers are happy because they assume they are buying goods at discounted prices, which indeed they are not. Another misleading approach in some department stores is when they claim that, for instance, a particular section of men's clothing is 25 percent off when in reality it is not, or it is discounted at 15 percent off. Most customers rely on the credibility of the store and do not check their receipts.

There is another category of misleading pricing techniques. When I look at the automotive section of a local newspaper I see many misleading messages. A dealership may say "Huge savings, up to ten thousand dollars off, this weekend only." It seems like an attractive deal, but by saying "up to," the dealership could offer a discount of only a few hundred dollars when you buy a car from them.

An advertisement with large letters indicates that "For only three days you will receive unbelievable savings." A new car that costs $25,000.00 is only $18,999.00. First, notice that this price is only one dollar short of $19,000, but more appealing. An asterisk next to the advertised price directs the readers to the bottom of the page. In very small letters that are hard to read or even to see, there is a list of many exclusions that are normally least expected, like dealer's preparations and undercoating.

While writing this part of the book, I went to a supermarket to buy fruits and vegetables. As I was walking in the produce section, I noticed several piles of apples of different colors next to one another. I looked at the prices of the first few piles of apples, which were priced fairly per pound. I filled a bag with apples that were in the middle of other piles of apples. When I was paying the cashier for my purchases, I realized that the total price was more than I expected. Before driving away, I reviewed the receipt and I noticed that price paid for that bag of apples was quite high because the apples were sold per unit and not per pound. I returned to the store to verify the mistake, and this is what I found. There were about seven kinds of apples. The price of each pile of apples was per pound, except for one pile. I was thinking as to why each kind of apple piled in one row sold per pound, with one exception? Was it a coincidence? What do you think?

Speaking of supermarkets and strategically placed items. Often, items are placed on the shelves in a way that maximizes their exposure for sales. Among many, the following are three sample approaches:

First, necessary items such as bread, dairy products, meat, and vegetables are all placed as far as possible from one another. The idea is that to purchase these items, one must pass by all aisles in the store, which increases the chance that one will buy more of less important items. Second, more expensive products are placed closer to our eyes and reach. Items with less marginal profits are placed on the lower shelves. For children, because of their height, more expensive items are on the lower shelves to increase their exposure. Third, convenience products, such as chewing gum and newspapers, are placed close to the cashiers. While waiting, we are more prone to purchase these low-priced items.

In the following section, we will examine advertisements (a term that I use interchangeably with "commercials") and brand labeling in international settings that failed to provide intended messages.

Hidden Agenda It was a few weeks ago that I visited a friend of mine, Fred, at his home during his recuperation from total hip surgery. We were drinking coffee and chatting while snow fell like powder, covering the ground. During my visit, the telephone next to him started to ring and a talking caller ID announced that his physiotherapist was on the line. Thinking that Fred did not want interruptions, I asked him to answer the phone at once, as it was an important call for him. He smiled and said, "At first I was thinking the same way." He continued by saying, "They wanted to perform physiotherapy more than was recommended. At first I said to myself that they are such caring people, but I found out that the more they visit me, the more they can charge the insurance company. I don't know if they are physiotherapists or telemarketers."

There was a time that full trust was given to most professionals because it was assumed that they wanted the best for us. It seems that this view is becoming a misunderstanding, as many of them think more of their own ends than for what is best for their clients. There have been, for example, many cases of unnecessary surgery done on patients, insurance agents who want to sell more insurance coverage than is needed, and representatives of private schools who call students with annoying frequency to get them to register.

Unintentional Ambiguity in Marketing

More than one might expect, there is a wide range of unintentional misunderstanding in promotional efforts, notably in advertising. For instance, I have come across an advertisement picture that shows a living room where family and friends are gathered. It becomes difficult to understand the purpose of such an advertisement. Would it be the floor carpeting, the living room furniture, or the designer outfits that the picture is trying to promote? The advertisement fails to emphasize the intended product clearly. Some promotional experts, however, believe that they are deliberate, in order to entice the viewers' curiosity.

The probability of creating a less effective or even countereffective advertisement is considerably higher in international settings. The underlining reason for this is that promotional planners overlook cultural variations from one market to another. As stated in *Marketing Week*, "It is quite an art to tweak the content and presentation of advertising in different countries to produce a universally acceptable message."[1] Kitcatt Nohr, as an example, advertised in England, showing pet owners hugging their pets. This advertisement lost its effectiveness in Italy because it is not common there to hug pets.[2]

Therefore, assuming cultural uniformity across nations creates misunderstandings that diminish promotional effectiveness.

Timotei Shampoo started selling their products in Taiwan, showing advertisements with a picture of a blond-haired woman. The Taiwanese women did not feel comfortable using the brand because they mainly have black hair. Later, the brand made the appropriate change to fit the market perception.[3]

It is also essential to be mindful of the meaning of words, brand names, and slogans across cultures. For example, Chevrolet, a division of General Motors, expanded the sales of its Nova to some of the Spanish-speaking countries, including Mexico. In their initial market entry, they noticed people's reluctance to buy the Nova, which probably occurred because in Spanish, "no" means "no," and "va" means "go."

If an advertising campaign is successful in one market, it does not guarantee its success in another market, despite considerable cultural similarities and shared language. Electrolux launched a successful advertising campaign in England with the slogan, "Nothing Sucks Like an Elecrolux." However, in the United Stated, the message was interpreted based on its colloquial meaning.[4]

Some years ago, I had consulted for an American shoe manufacturer who wanted to explore the Western European markets for exports. The company specialized in men's shoes with thick soles. The initial plan was to disseminate catalogs and samples of its shoes to prospective intermediaries and major department stores. Although the company was successful in the American market, I advised more studies before implementing their plan. The reason was that a major portion of the American market prefers men's shoes with relatively thick soles that signify quality. However, Western European men favor thin soles on their shoes. Therefore, the manufacturer was looking into the possibility of adapting to that market by making shoes with thin soles or to exploring other markets.

Commercials

Effective commercial campaigns are critically important; otherwise, they will lead to failures and disappointments. This section will discuss major components of successful commercials, mainly related to global settings.

Taking into Account Norms and Expectations of Viewers Marketing messages must be in harmony with the norms and expectations of the target market. For example, in general, Japanese, compared with Europeans and North Americans, prefer to see a commercial that mostly generates feelings rather than facts.[5] So that in Japan, advertisements about the performance and price of a product, particularly those that concern comparison with the competition, are not a common practice.[6] Therefore, if a commercial is successful in the United States, that does not secure the same results in Japan.

What makes the matter more complex is that music in an advertisement may evoke different feelings and sentiments from one cultural setting to another. A soft drink company advertised its product with hip-hop and rap music in a few industrialized countries. The campaign resulted in great success. The soft drink company decided to continue with the same approach in one of the emerging markets. Soon it realized that the customers preferred native traditional music in the advertisements.

Regard for Legal Aspects of Commercials
Launching a commercial campaign in a new market necessitates careful inquiry into legal constraints.

As an illustration, in 1973, the Federal Trade Commission clarified that comparative advertisement is not an unfair practice.[7] However, in many countries, including some in Western Europe, comparing one brand with another is prohibited.

Which products can or cannot be advertised is also an important consideration. J. Thomas Russell and W. Ronald Lane pointed out that "For example, fresh eggs may not be advertised in France, and cruise advertising is not allowed in Italy." [8]

Marketers should also be cognizant of nudity or messages with sexual connotations in their advertisements. The extent to which these approaches can be practiced varies significantly across countries.

Decision-Making Process
In almost any book on management or organizational behavior, a section is devoted to centralized and decentralized decision making. From an organizational perspective, centralized decision making refers to the authority to make decisions by one or a few individuals. Contrary to this is decentralized decision making, in which delegation of authority takes place. This is when decision makers pass on power to others at a lower echelon in the organization.

Centralized decision making has its own advantages. It delivers more uniformity of delivered goods and services. It also provides a better way to monitor pertinent performances and take corrective actions as needed. Moreover, it is a device to minimize duplication of the work process.

On the other hand, decentralized decision making delivers its own advantages, among which the following can be stated. Decentralized decision making involves entrusting those who are involved in the work process with the authority to make decisions. That could help boost employee morale and motivation. Also, as a rule of thumb, decisions made by several individuals instead of one or a few individuals deliver better results.

In the case of promotional strategies in international landscapes, decentralized decision making has an underlying advantage. It is advisable to delegate the authority to make decisions to the local subsidiaries, rather than those decisions emanating from the headquarters. The reason is that decisions can be made and implemented more efficiently by those who are more familiar with the local market. It is a particularly invaluable approach when a quick response to the competition, such as in pricing, is needed.

Appropriate Translation More and more, international corporations are relying on well-thought-out translations of a slogan or a message in order to prevent distorted meanings.

There is also a growing expansion of organizations that specialize in translation. Through both secondary and then primary research, they concern themselves with the meanings of a given message among various cultures.

Per Capita Income and Level of Literacy

There are a host of considerations in advertisement campaigns. The credibility of a given channel of advertisement is one thing that should be taken into account. For example, sending coupons or notices of sales to individuals is known as direct marketing by the marketers, whereas it is mostly known by the receivers as junk mail, which is placed in the trash can. At this point, we refer to two important matters related to the effectiveness of advertisements.

Per Capita Income There have been frequent situations in which marketing decisions have failed to take into account the purchasing power of their target market and have subsequently realized unfavorable outcomes in their commercial campaign. In many countries, the average yearly income per individual is less than $2,000.00. In such markets, advertisements for large packages of specific products or advertisements for expensive items may lose effectiveness.

With respect to per capita income, it is important to note that, for example, country A might have a higher per capita income than country B. But country B could be a more suitable market because of its higher purchasing ability. Why? It is because of the favorable monetary exchange rates and the pricing structures of that market. Therefore, it is important to look into both per capita income and the purchasing power of that given market.

Literacy Rate Another important element to consider is the literacy level of the target market. Advertising with written descriptions might only be suitable in markets with a high literacy rate. In environments in which there is a low rate of literacy, written advertisements lose their effectiveness and, hence, should be in visual forms, such as billboards or similar channels of advertisements.

Concluding Points

Often a major portion of marketing investment is allocated to promotional activities. Yet, it has always been a thorny task to measure and conclude the specific level of effectiveness of such activities. One thing is clear: promotional efforts are complicated, particularly with respect to international marketing. Considering a new market without ample knowledge of its socio-cultural and other environmental conditions is like walking in the dark in an unknown area. Therefore, a promotional campaign for a new market should be crafted with care to minimize the risk of unwanted consequences. In the next chapter I will discuss issues, concepts, and potential misunderstandings in negotiations.

ENDNOTES

1. "Overseas Media: Becoming worldly-wise," *Marketing Week,* June 17, 2004, p. 43. http://proquest.umi.com

2. *Ibid.*

3. David Kilburn, "Crossing Border. (Advertising Foreign Brand Products in Asia)," *Adweek,* April 14, 1997, pp. 22, 24.

4. Michael R. Czinkota, and Ilkka A. Ronkainen, *International Marketing,* 6th ed. (Fort Worth: Harcourt, 2001), p. 65.

5. Kate Gillespie, Jean-Pierre Jeannet, and H. David Hennessy, *Global Marketing: An Interactive Approach* (Boston: Houghton Mifflin Company, 2004), p. 418.

6. *Ibid.*

7. J. Thomas Russell and W. Ronald Lane, *Kleppner's Advertising Procedure,* 12th ed. (Englewood Cliffs, NJ: Prentice Hall, 1993), p. 474.

8. *Ibid,* p. 656.

RECOMMENDED READING

Kenneth E. Clow and Donald Baack. *Integrated Advertising, Promotion, and Marketing Communications.* Upper Saddle River, NJ: Pearson Education, 2007.

Louis E. Boone and David L. Kurtz. *Contemporary Marketing.* Mason, OH: South-Western, 2006.

Michael J. Etzel, Bruce J. Walker, and William J. Stanton, *Marketing.* New York: McGraw Hill/Irwin, 2007.

Philip Kotler and Kevin Lane Keller. *Marketing Management.* Upper Saddle River, NJ: Pearson Education, 2006.

Philip R. Cateora and John L. Graham. *International Marketing.* New York: McGraw Hill/ Irwin, 2007.

Subhash C. Jain. *International Marketing Management.* Cincinnati: South-Western College Publishing, 1996.

Warren J. Keegan and Mark C. Green. *Global Marketing.* Upper Saddle River, NJ: Pearson Prentice Hall, 2005.

William Well, John Burnett, and Sandra Moriarty. *Advertising: Principles and Practice.* Upper Saddle River, NJ: Pearson Education, 2003.

CHAPTER SIX

GLOBAL NEGOTIATIONS, PROTOCOLS, AND MARKET ENTRY

Consider someone who is driving in a residential neighborhood and sees a garage sale. The driver stops the car and walks toward the many items for sale. While he is looking at different bargains, he notices an attractive antique lamp, which he finds quite appropriate for one of the rooms of his house. The price is higher than he wants to pay. He begins to negotiate with the seller and succeeds in purchasing the lamp for a very attractive price.

Negotiations take place in many other situations as well; for instance, when a patient negotiates with a physician's assistant to set a convenient date and time for an appointment, or when two parties become involved in a negotiation for a time of their meeting. Negotiation also takes place between an employee and the human resources department of the organization over salary and benefits. Or, it can be seen when a young boy bargains with the parents for a later bedtime.

In this chapter, I will present two broad areas of misunderstanding. One is the view that all negotiations are based on the notion of a zero-sum game, meaning that in order for someone to gain, someone else has to lose. The other source of misunderstanding in negotiation is pertinent to cross-cultural settings. Too often business negotiators assume that because a given approach produced a successful result in their home country, it will be effective in host countries as well. In this chapter I will also provide a number of case studies to deepen our understanding of the nature and dynamics of negotiations. Finally, I will open a section to show many dos and don'ts of negotiations in cross-cultural landscapes.

The Two Broad Categories of Negotiation

Mono-Locus Approach The mono-locus approach is when one side or each side of a negotiation tries to gain as much as possible at the bargaining table with no or minimal concern for the other party. Such an approach often prevents long-term relationships and impedes future negotiations.

An East Coast Oriental rug and antique merchant shared the following with me to describe his strategy to purchase various items for next to nothing. He related that recently an individual walked into his store carrying a rug of about 5 x 8 feet on his shoulder and was anxious to sell it. Although the merchant needed a carpet like that, he told him, "I am overstocked with this type of carpet. But in order to help you out, I can make you an offer," which he did. The man gave it some thought and reluctantly accepted it. While the seller was waiting for a check, the merchant looked at the carpet again, and told him, "Oh, I did not see this hole in the carpet and these imperfections."

The merchant explained to me that the hole could have been fixed very easily, and those imperfections were expected with handmade carpets. In fact, it is one way to differentiate between handmade and machine-made carpets. The merchant further stated that he knew the condition of the carpet at the very beginning, when he first glanced at it, but pretended he did not as an approach to lower the sales price even further. He said to the seller, "I cannot buy it for the price that I quoted you, considering these flaws that I did not notice earlier." Finally the desperate seller agreed on a lower price, and the deal was completed. Soon after, the merchant sold it for a hefty profit.

The same merchant also shared the following. He occasionally receives telephone calls from those who want to exchange their old carpets for new ones. Often, these old carpets are rare antiques. He told me "I received a similar call only a few days ago from an elderly woman. As per her request, I went to her home because she had a few antique carpets that she wanted to get rid of in exchange for new wall-to-wall carpeting, and I agreed to help her. She did not seem to be aware that for a fraction of the value of one of her antique carpets, she would be able to get wall-to-wall carpeting for her home."

Edward de Bono in his book *The New Think* elaborates on the importance and benefits of creative thinking. He provided a case, explaining how a young woman was able to outsmart a cunning merchant through her creativity.[1]

Poly-Locus Approach In a poly-locus approach, negotiation is based on reciprocal consideration and open communication between all parties. The main ingredient is fairness, which leads to satisfaction and long-term relationships between the involved parties.

One of the largest accounting firms in the Washington, D.C. area was, for several years, undertaking the tax preparation for a well-known entertainment company with many branches nationwide. The fees for the tax preparation were about $300,000.00. Each year the accounting firm added about 5 percent to its fees to offset the inflation rate and to account for the expansion of the entertainment company.

For tax preparation for 2005, the top management executives of both the accounting firm and the entertainment company held a meeting. The purpose of the meeting was for the entertainment company executives to explain that for the first time in eight years, they had had a bad financial year. Not only did their income not increase, but it was lower than initially forecasted. Therefore, they were requesting to pay not the usual 5 percent increase in tax preparation fees; additionally, the entertainment company wanted to pay a rate comparable to the fee they had paid two years ago. Their rationale was that the company needed to save money and cut costs as much as reasonably possible to create a base for future growth.

After a relatively short meeting between both sides in the negotiations, the accounting firm agreed to make an exception by going along with the request of its client.

Luckily, the entertainment company was able to return to its usual growth path in 2006, and subsequently, the accounting firm received its 5 percent increase, plus an additional surcharge as compensation for the previous year.

The following occurrence, which I witnessed, describes how one can create a winning situation for both sides. It was only a few weeks ago that I walked into one of the chain car-rental stores to rent a vehicle. I noticed a customer ahead of me saying to a representative that he was not happy with the car he rented the day before because the air conditioning was not working properly. He added that as a result, it would be difficult for him and his family to keep the car until the next day, when they were scheduled to drop the car off at BWI airport.

The representative, John, could have responded in the following ways:

- He could say that there is not much that can be done because the air conditioning was working properly at the time of rental, and it is now the customer's responsibility.

- He could tell the customer to fill up the gas tank and bring the car back, and then give him a similar car.

- He could charge the customer for the consumed gas and give him a similar car on the spot.

However, John took a different approach in responding to the customer, which went like this:

John: "I am sorry for the inconvenience, and for that I am going to give you our most luxurious automobile instead of another midsized car."

Customer: "Really?"

John: "Yes sir!"

Customer: "You are not going to charge me more for the exchanged car?"

John: "No, we are not going to charge you any more than you were going to pay."

Customer: "How about the gas tank that is half full? Do you want me to fill up the car and bring it back?"

John: "That is not necessary. We will take care of it for you."

I saw a big smile of satisfaction on the customer's face.

After John helped that customer, he gave me a ride home because I returned my rental. Having known John for about two years, I felt comfortable asking him this question on the way: What was his reason for his overly gracious gesture to that customer? He commented that there is nothing better than having happy customers in such a competitive business, especially when it does not cost you a penny. I asked him for a further explanation. John responded that luxury cars are expectedly much more expensive to rent, and because of that, there is much less demand for them. He added that that particular car had been in their lot for a few days, and as a result they were losing money each day. John added that such cars, however, have more demand when they are at the airport. "Knowing that we did not have anybody to take that car back to the airport, my offer to that customer made us both happy, and what's better than that?"

The following describes a condition of multidimensional winning. Some years ago I was in Colorado, where I became acquainted with a merchant of men's clothing. On one occasion the shared an intriguing experience with me about the creativity of an independent wholesaler.

At one time the wholesaler contacted the merchant wanting to sell several large boxes containing designer shirts and accessories for men. The merchant expressed his interest in buying the merchandise, but he could not. He had many small-size shirts which he could not sell. On one hand, he did not have adequate space to place more shirts; on the other, hand he did not want to spend more on something which was risky to sell.

The wholesaler noticed all the shirts that the merchant could not sell were in a small size, as the medium, large, and extra large sizes were already sold.

Relying on his problem solving ability and creativity, the wholesaler proposed that he would be willing to buy all these leftover shirts if the merchant bought the boxes containing designer shirts and accessories. The fact was that the wholesaler knew an international trader who was looking for small –size shirts to export to one of the Asian countries where on the average, men are smaller in height than American men.

The negotiation resulted in satisfaction and profit making for the international trader, the wholesaler, and the merchant.

No Room for Negotiation

In this section you will notice two cases of negotiation. One of them is a case of understanding between the two parties that resulted in a done deal. The later is a case of unsuccessful negotiation as a result of misunderstanding.

The Purchasing of an Antique Painting Mrs. M., who was from a wealthy family, was looking for several months for a special type of antique painting for her living room. One day when she was visiting a series of antique stores, surprisingly, she came across exactly what she was looking for.

Mrs. M. contacted her uncle who was a well-known and well-respected expert in antique items, including paintings. She wanted his opinion about the quality and originality of the painting, and she wanted to know what would be a fair price for it.

Through an arrangement, Mrs. M. asked her uncle, Mr. Z., and the owner of the antique shop to meet at her house. The owner of the store, Mr. N., was going to bring the painting with him to show to both Mrs. M. and her uncle, Mr. Z.

On the designated afternoon, Mr. N. arrived with two men who were carrying the painting. After the usual greetings, Mrs. M. enthusiastically said to her uncle, "This is the painting I was telling you about. What do you think?"

Mr. Z. was such an expert in antique paintings that he did not even care to examine the painting closely. All he said to Mrs. M was, "Do you have your checkbook with you?" She said, "Yes, here it is."

Mr. Z. quietly told her how much she should write the check for, and she promptly complied. Mr. Z. asked the store owner to come forward to receive the check for the purchase of the painting. Mr. N. saw the check and politely commented that the amount was much less than he expected, and that it would not even cover his cost.

Implying that there was no room for negotiation and that it was a done deal, Mr. Z. said, "Have a good day; have a good day," implying that it was time for them to leave, which they did. Mr. N. thanked Mrs. M. and her uncle, and left with his two employees, who had carried the painting to the house.

Note that the seller did not set the price, but Mr. Z. did. Mr. Z. was confident that the seller not only covered his costs, but also made a fair profit. Knowing about Mr. Z.'s expertise and negotiation skills, the seller was aware that any attempt to bargain would have been a waste of time and would probably risk the sale of the painting all together.

Bargaining in a Department Store

In many societal scenes around the world, almost everything for sale is subject to negotiation. In fact, negotiation is not only a way to determine a mutually acceptable price between the seller and the buyer, but it is also a means of socialization and a way to create customer loyalty.

A young man who came to the United States to study at a university went to a department store to buy a few things for himself and his newly rented apartment. While walking in the men's shoe department, he noticed a pair of shoes that he was interested in. He found a salesperson and their exchange went like this.

Customer: "Do you have a pair of shoes like this, size half-past nine?"

The salesperson smiled and asked: "Do you mean nine-and-a-half?"

Customer: "Sorry, yes that is what I mean."

Salesperson: "Yes, we do."

The customer tried them on and asked for the price.

Salesperson: "They are $129.00"

Customer: "That's too much money for a pair of shoes! How about if I give you $30.00 for this pair?"

Salesperson: "Sir, our prices are fixed, we cannot give discounts"

Customer: "You are a hard negotiator. Ok, I'll give you $50.00 for them."

Salesperson: "Our prices are fixed."

Customer: "This is my last offer, $75.00. I cannot go any higher than that."

Salesperson: "Sir, our prices are fixed, we are not allowed to give any discount."

Finally, the young man, who was not accustomed to buying something without negotiation and receiving some type of discount, had no choice but to pay the full price or simply not purchase the shoes.

He gave some thought to it and reluctantly agreed to pay the full price for the shoes.

The salesperson added the 6 percent sales tax and asked the customer to pay $136.74.

The customer, who was not familiar with a sales tax, became puzzled by the new price. He asked, "Why can you not lower the price, but for one reason or another you can raise the price? That is not right; you are trying to take advantage of me for liking the shoes by asking for more."

The young man was quite disenchanted because of the unsuccessful negotiation. He walked away without buying the shoes.

Negotiation is a strategically oriented art, and it should be handled with care. Otherwise, it could lead to conflict and misunderstanding, particularly when entering into a different cultural setting. This section will address many of these conditions.

Instrumentality and Terminality of Negotiation

Many business negotiations are destined to fail because some corporate negotiators are concerned about time efficiency, or "getting to the point," as relevant to the instrumentality of the negotiation. However, others are more concerned with the terminality, or outcome of the negotiation. This approach is commonly embedded in establishing both trust and a sound interpersonal relationship between parties in a negotiation. It is believed that negotiation without establishing a trusting relationship is like constructing a building with a shallow foundation. Such construction is more prone to breakdown. Terminality oriented negotiation is a way to ensure mutually beneficial future transactions.

M. Katherine Glover asserted that, "Many nationalities value the personal relationship more than most Americans do in business. In these countries, long-term relationships based on trust are necessary for conducting business. Many U.S. firms make the mistake of rushing into business discussions...."[2] Many negotiators in Scandinavian countries and Canada prefer efficiency of process. However, most transactions in Egypt, Mexico, Japan, China, and the United Arab Emirates are based on terminality. Regarding the importance of interpersonal relationships in China for negotiation, Dave Archer notes that "The better your relationship, the better chance you have of negotiating a viable agreement that benefits both parties."[3]

When one party exhibits more concern about the instrumentality of the negotiation and the other party focuses on its terminality, this in itself leads to what I call "tempo differentiation" of the process, which potentially leads to transaction breakdown. One party may perceive that their counternegotiators just want to "get down to business" and make a deal. The other part, may perceive the situation differently, that their counternegotiators are not really serious, or for one reason or another, they want to delay the deal.

Types of Connectivity in Negotiation
There are three approaches to negotiation in terms of connectivity and involvement.

First, there are some negotiators who pay full attention to what is being said by the other party. They also want to make sure that they are exhibiting their attention by refraining from doing anything but listening. Also, they occasionally rephrase what has been conveyed. This approach, on a reciprocal basis, can lead to successful outcomes.

Second, there are some negotiators who also pay full attention to what is being communicated by the other negotiator but meanwhile might be doing something else, such as looking at some papers or files. Periodically, they might say, "Go on, I am listening to you." This approach is grounds for misunderstanding because one party in negotiation is listening to the other one, but exhibiting behavior that sends a different message.

Third, there are some negotiators who pretend to be listening carefully, although their thoughts are elsewhere. More than seldom, a negotiator who is not paying attention to both verbal and nonverbal messages, such as the tone of voice or facial expressions of the other party, is thinking of a response instead. One can imagine the outcomes of such a negotiation, in which each party, in lieu of being concerned with the comments and nonverbal cues of the counterpart, is only thinking of a comment in response.

Diverse Protocols and Beyond

In a business transaction, the two parties gather with good intentions geared toward successful results. However, a behavior or protocol that is common in one culture may be improper in another, which interferes with effective negotiation. In this section, I will evaluate a number of these conditions.

The Art of Handshakes There is much more to a handshake than what may appear. There are variations of handshakes with regard to their firmness, duration, and frequency. In the Middle East, for instance, handshakes are normally given with minimal firmness, but they occur quite frequently and with a short grip. In France, and some other European countries, handshakes are relatively less frequent than in the Middle East. They are firm, with a short grip. In the United States, handshakes are least frequent, but they are quite firm and have a longer duration.

Lack of knowledge regarding the variation of handshakes from one country to another is a cause of misinterpretation. For instance, a warm handshake by one party may be taken as lack of interest by another party.

Preparation of Documents and Their Submission for Signature The content of any contract needs to be crystal clear before being brought to the table for signatures to prevent any potential embarrassment or legal complications. The format of the contract is also significantly important. For example, some negotiators want to place their signature immediately after the content of the contract comes to an end, without leaving any blank space. This is to prevent the possibility of the other party in negotiation adding more to the content of the contract in blank spaces above the signatures.

Another matter of importance is whether to exchange documents with the left or right hand. In some cultures, the left hand is for personal hygiene and should not be used for handling papers.

Often, communication concerning transactions or negotiation is via e-mail. In some countries a delay in response is quite typical and should not necessarily be interpreted as a lack of interest.

Using the First or the Last Name?

In the United States, using first names is quite frequent among colleagues and co-workers. Americans commonly prefer to use someone's first name after the first or a few meetings. It is perceived as a gesture of closeness and friendship. On the other hand, Japanese, Germans, and French adhere to use of the last name for a much longer period of time as a matter of protocol in formal organizations.

A few years ago, an American entertainment company was in the process of entering into a joint-venture agreement with a Japanese firm. The American company invited a team from the Japanese firm to come from Tokyo to San Francisco for further negotiation. For the event, the first names of the attendees were written on identification tags.

Upon the return of the Japanese team to their corporate headquarters, a letter was sent to the head of the American company. Aside from their appreciation of the hospitality they received, they expressed their disenchantment over the use of their first names.

Dates on Documents and Letters

Another source of confusion is that in one country, such as Switzerland, when writing dates it is customary to first write the day, then the month, and then the year. In another country, namely, the United States, it is customary to write the month, then the day, and then the year. Such a difference can create a lot of misunderstandings in terms of dates for meetings or contract signing.

Variations in the Customs and Protocols

Knowledge of the customs and protocols of the people with whom we are interacting is important to minimizing misinterpretations. Below is a sample of these variations.

- When making a point, Italians move their hands more frequently than the Japanese.

- In Saudi Arabia, it is rude to cross one's legs in a way that shows the bottoms of the shoes; in some other countries crossing legs is a condition of informality.

- It is important to be on time in Germany and in Switzerland, whereas being about a half hour late in most South American countries is acceptable.

- In Iran, the bottom layer of the cooked rice, which is crisp and crunchy, is served to the guests as the best part of the rice, whereas in Pakistan the top layer part of the cooked rice is considered the best part.

- French negotiators welcome negotiations over lunch, whereas Americans prefer to talk about business after lunch. Also, having lunch takes less time in the United States than in France or other parts of Europe.

- Beer is served at room temperature in most parts of Europe, including Belgium, England, and Austria, whereas it is mostly served chilled in the United States.

- Americans often have salad before their dinner, whereas the Swiss and most other Europeans have it served with their main course.

- In the United States, bouquets are made with an even number of flowers, often a dozen, but in Scandinavian countries, they are arranged with odd numbers.

- In China, unlike most other countries, sneezing should not be noticed by others.

Misunderstanding in Global Market Entry

Doing business in other countries can be both challenging and rewarding. A common concept is that because one type of market entry is successful in one country for a given product, it will have the same outcome in other countries. In most cases such concepts are misleading because of differences in socio-cultural, economic, demographic, technological, geographical, political, legal, as well as competitive conditions across markets. There are many forms of market entry, such as licensing and franchising, turnkey projects, contract manufacturing, management contracting, and foreign direct investment (FDI). FDI can be in the form of joint-venture agreements or wholly owned subsidiaries. In this section, I will identify and comment on various pitfalls in the latter type of FDI because often the wholly owned subsidiaries carry both a higher risk and profit than other types of market entry.

Pitfalls in International Wholly Owned Subsidiaries Among the thorniest pitfalls in a new-market entry are the ways a product is perceived in that given market, the level of political stability of the host country, the concept and the meaning of ownership, and the issue of bribery.

Perception of Foreign Products In
some cultures, people are attracted to foreign products because they see them as exotic or at least different. On the other hand, in some other cultures the notion of ethnocentrism or cultural superiority persists. In such cultures, negotiations and the distribution of foreign products becomes exceedingly cumbersome.

Political Stability The issues of confis-
cation and expropriation must not be overlooked. Both mean governmental takeover. Confiscation is a transfer of ownership without compensation, whereas expropriation is transfer of ownership with some sort of compensation. When there is a history of political instability in a country, FDI becomes a very risky business. The marketer should consider other types of entry, such as exports to that country, in order to minimize the risk of loss of assets.

Bribery This is indeed a challenging matter
that can cause considerable misunderstandings. In many societies, bribery is unethical and even illegal, whereas in some others places it is a conventional practice. One explanation for this is the inadequacy of salaries of governmental officials in some countries or provinces. Therefore, bribery is a means of supplemental income. Bribery is bending the rules in favor of a party who offers money. We may note two other similar practices. extortion, which is when a government representative makes things difficult for someone to lawfully pursue legal rights, such as obtaining the permit to construct an apartment building, unless adequate payment is directed to a given official. Finally, lubrication can be mentioned,

which refers to a tip or small sum of money given to someone at a lower echelon in order to expedite or facilitate a process; for instance, by placing a specific file at the top of other files for immediate priority process.

Marketing Research

In order to minimize the risk of ownership or control over the operations of a subsidiary, one must conduct a feasibility study, which can be done through secondary and primary research.

Secondary research is relatively efficient and much less costly than primary research. Secondary research is comprised of reading governmental and other publications regarding the feasibility of entering into a given market. Such exploration includes finding the level of demand for a given product, the level of competition, and the condition of a particular economic infrastructure.

It should not be overlooked that too often the collected data is either outdated or inaccurate, which is more evident in developing countries. In some cases, a given government may deliberately publish inaccurate data to signify more favorable conditions for various reasons, namely, to attract foreign investments. Should the secondary research offer a favorable outlook, the marketer should consider the inclusion of primary research.

Primary research can be by the means of face-to-face interviews with the people in a particular market, telephone surveys, or valid and reliable survey questionnaires. Although the primary research approach generates more updated and more accurate data than secondary research, it has its own share of potential for misunderstandings.

- Face-to-face data gathering can deviate from accuracy because of perceptual differences. For example, "a lot of snowfall" may not mean the same thing in Boulder, Colorado, as it does in Key West, Florida.

- Surveys via telephone in one culture may seem conventional, but in another culture they may be considered as obscene phone calls. Therefore, the receiver of the phone call may not respond or may deliberately provide inaccurate information.

- Written questionnaires can be troublesome because in many societies most people cannot write or read their own native language. Additionally, many questions can be considered too personal or even offensive. Therefore, respondents may not want to answer these questions, or at least not with accuracy.

Final Notes

Knowledge of the negotiation process involving a party of another culture and business protocols is significantly important when entering a new market. Knowledge of the advantages and disadvantages of each type of market entry is equally important. Also, learning about the external environment is another critical dimension of going forward on the path to success. In addition to what I have presented already, many other conditions need to be scrutinized, such as the practices of imposing protective tariffs, quotas, subsidies, and embargoes as major barriers to international trade. Also, when entering a new market, it is important to learn about the rates of inflation, labor laws, salaries, and similar pertinent matters, especially per capita income and its distribution pattern for that market.

ENDNOTES

1. Edward de Bono, *The New Think: The Use of Lateral Thinking in the Generation of New Ideas*, 2nd impression (New York: Basic Books, 1968).

2. M. Katherine Glover, "Do's & Taboos: Cultural Aspects of International Business," *Business America*, August 13, 1990, p. 3.

3. Dave Archer, "Doing Business in China," *The Journal of Commerce*, October 30, 2006, p. 64.

RECOMMENDED READING

Charles Hill. *Global Business Today*. New York: McGraw Hill/Irwin, 2008.

Paul R. Krugman and Maurice Obstfeld. *International Economics: Theory & Policy*. Boston: Pearson Addison Wesley, 2009.

Scot Ober. *Contemporary Business Communication*. Boston: Houghton Mifflin Company, 2001.

Sondra Thiederman, *Profiting in America's Multicultural Marketplace: How to Do Business Across Cultural Lines*. Lanham, MD: Lexington Books, 1992.

Ricky W. Griffin and Michael W. Pustay. *International Business: A Managerial Perspective*. Upper Saddle River, NJ: Pearson Prentice Hall, 2005.

Terri Morrison, Wayne A. Conaway, and George A. Borden. *How to Do Business in Sixty Countries: Kiss, Bow, or Shake Hands*. Holbrook, MA: 1994.

CHAPTER SEVEN

CONDITIONS AND COMMUNICATION

To deepen our understanding of the nature and types of misunderstanding, I will present a set of related cases. First, there are two incidents of misunderstanding on my part that I will describe. Second, I will present a case of self-misunderstanding, in which an individual does not recognize one's own full potential in certain domains. Third, I will explain the meaning of success, effective leadership, norms in conflict resolution, and the emphasis on teamwork versus competition that varies in cross-cultural settings. Fourth, I will discuss the complexity of communication in international environments. Finally, I will outline several guidelines for minimizing misunderstanding among people of different cultural backgrounds, some of which will set implications for successful communication within a culture.

Luckily It Did Not Happen

I have already discussed a range of cases of misunderstanding, including those which have occurred in managerial activities, in business settings, and in marketing decisions. In this section I present two cases of my misunderstanding that were close to causing unpleasant results, but luckily, did not. This is to demonstrate the ease with which one can fall onto the path of misunderstanding.

Where Is My Pen? A few years ago I was taking a KLM flight from Schiphol airport in Amsterdam to Dulles airport in Washington, D.C. I was sitting next to the window. On my right, there was an empty seat that separated me from a middle-aged and professional-looking man. We were served lunch, and shortly after, with my black Mont Blanc pen, I started to make a list of the things I needed to do in the next few days. While writing, I felt drowsy and ended up taking a short nap. When I opened my eyes, I noticed my pen was missing; I had had it in my hand before taking a nap. Unsuccessfully, I looked everywhere around my seat, on the floor, around my feet, and in my pockets, but could not find it.

While thinking where else my pen might be, I noticed that the man on my right was using my pen. I did not know how to react or what to say to him. In this predicament, several possible alternatives passed through my mind. Should I ask him to give me back my pen or should I complain to a flight attendant? Complain about what—tell the attendant that he has my pen without my permission? If he denies it, then how could I prove that it is my pen? Or, should I wait until we arrive at the airport and then speak with an airline representative?

While thinking about these alternatives, I started to have a very brief conversation with him, which was similar to this:

"Is this a Mont Blanc?" I asked.

"Yes it is," he replied.

While looking at the pen, I asked him, "How long are you going to use it?" He did not know how to respond to my odd question, as he probably thought I was trying to begin a conversation with him.

"Well, probably as long as I need it," he responded.

By then I knew my questions were futile, and that I might make the matter worse by continuing to question him. A few minutes later, I saw that he finished writing and had placed the pen in his jacket pocket. Seeing this did not help the situation.

Upon arrival at the airport, passengers began to pick up their belongings to leave the plane. I waited while others left the plane because I wanted to speak with a flight attendant or a representative concerning my experience. While waiting, I bent down to pick up my briefcase from under my seat. Most unexpectedly, I saw my pen, which was "hiding" behind my briefcase. Apparently, when I was taking a nap the pen fell from my hand.

Hesitantly, I rushed to leave the plane to find the man so I could apologize to him and explain the situation but could not find him.

Too Close to Break a Relationship

Mr. P. was the general manager of an automotive dealership whom I happened to know for over fifteen years. I always had pleasant experiences negotiating with him, to the extent that I recommended him to my close friends. About six months ago, I went to the dealership to purchase a car. I found that Mr. P. was no longer working there but that he was with a nearby dealership. I went to the other dealership, and there he was. But Mr. P. was not the general manager; he was the director of finance. He kindly introduced me to the general manager and the sales manager of the dealership. Through their help and collaborative negotiation, I was able to find a car with an attractive price.

I then had to go to Mr. P to take care of the paperwork. The purchase was without financing through the dealership. Among many papers that I had to fill out, there were a brief loan application, one for the credit check, and one for the proof of insurance coverage for the new purchase. Content with my purchase and confident in Mr. P.'s honesty, I was not concerned about signing the papers before me.

A couple of days after my purchase, I began to file my paperwork relating to my purchase, during which, ironically, I noticed that I had applied for a $4,900.00 loan. As a result, I drove to the dealership for clarification. When I showed the paper to Mr. P., he commented that the loan was meant for another customer and apologized for the confusion. Finally, the problem was resolved and the loan application was destroyed. This incident led me to become more cognizant concerning each of the papers I signed in the dealership. In this process, I could not understand why I gave the dealership permission to check my credit history and provided them with proof of insurance coverage for the automobile because I was not applying for a loan through them.

Three mistakes! That is a lot of mistakes for one purchase. I was quite uneasy about the whole thing. I wanted to find out about their motive for asking me to sign these irrelevant documents. With all of the paperwork with me, I drove to the dealership to complain to the general manager concerning my experience.

While I was driving, my cell phone rang. The caller was a sales manager from another dealership who said that he had just located the car I was looking for. I informed him that I had already purchased one. In the meantime, while I had him on line, I told him about my bizarre experience regarding the dealership's request for a credit check and proof of insurance coverage, when I had not applied for a loan. His response was that there is a new law that requires dealerships to check each buyer's credit and requires buyers to provide proof of insurance coverage, regardless of whether or not they are requesting a loan. I was very appreciative of his explanation.

I turned around and drove back home. While driving I was thinking about my misunderstanding, and how close I came to finding myself in a regretful and embarrassing situation.

Self-Misunderstanding

When we think of misunderstanding, generally it is about communication with someone, a condition, or an event. Misunderstanding can also be about ourselves or the potential that we possess. The following describes one of the most memorable events of my academic years.

About fifteen years ago I was teaching a basic management course at a four-year college. Occasionally, I had students whose tuition was paid by a not-for-profit organization. In such cases, I was asked to fill out a short report concerning a student's academic progress. The progress had to meet a minimum satisfactory level for tuition reimbursement.

In one of my classes, I had a student who was noticeably shy and withdrawn. Not so surprisingly, he earned grades below the satisfactory level. One day after class, when everyone had already left, he hesitantly brought his report card to me to fill out. I paused and said, "I hope you see the situation I am in. I cannot write that you are in good academic standing in my class while you are not. If I write about your low academic performance, then you will be faced with financial troubles."

As if he had an answer ready, he replied, "Just write down that I am not smart, as most other students. And, in fact my counselor thinks the same way about me...." I interrupted him by asking him several irrelevant questions, such as the name of his favorite elementary teacher. He successfully answered all of them.

Puzzled by my questions, he politely asked me the relevancy of my questions to his report card.

I replied "A lot! I see a contradiction here. If you were not so smart, then how could you remember the answers to these questions that I just asked you?"

The smile on his face and the glow in his eyes was unforgettable. He then came to recognize that he underestimated his ability to learn and comprehend.

I will never forget that this student earned one of the highest scores on the final exam.

In the remainder of this chapter, I will draw some conclusions and offer guidelines for minimizing misunderstandings.

Organizations and Cultural Diversity

Organizations are formed of individuals working coordinately and systematically toward a common organizational goal. There are many aspects of organizations that are subject to misunderstandings because of their variations across cultures. Below I discuss the meaning of success from one organizational setting to another, effective leadership, different approaches in managing conflicts, and views on teamwork.

Meaning of Success In some cultures success is measured by a person's level of income, whereas in other cultures success might equate with working for a multinational and globally known company. In some other cultural settings, longevity and affiliation with an organization indicate success because they indicate one's determination and stability. Yet, in some other settings, having more responsibility, being promoted, or having a sophisticated title signifies success.

Therefore, it becomes obvious that a given managerial approach for motivating employees that would be effective in one culture may become ineffective in another.

Leadership In some societies, managers are respected because they make decisions based on their knowledge and experience in such a way that affects employees and organizations. To maintain their respect, they must make decisions on their own and announce them. Therefore, soliciting input from employees signifies their lack of ability to make decisions independently. From another perspective, some employees argue that managers do not undertake part of their work, so they wonder why they should be involved in a manager's job, which is to make decisions and announce them. On the other hand, in some societies, employees strive for delegation of authority and participative decision making. In fact, this style of management is a major source of employee motivation.

Conflict Resolution Depending on cultural setting, there are distinct approaches in organizations dealing with interpersonal conflicts. For instance, in some organizations, the common practice is to bring conflicts into the open, either on a face-to-face basis, with the presence and involvement of the manager, or in a departmental meeting. People share and discuss their differences and seek a resolution, mostly without developing hard feelings toward each other. In some other cultures, active conflict resolution through openly discussing a matter results in losing face, regardless of the outcome. In other words, initiating an open discussion may intensify the existing conflict.

Therefore, it becomes clear that a manager of an organization who is accustomed to a given approach for resolving conflicts should be aware that such an approach may be counterproductive in a different setting.

Teamwork and Productivity Depending on a given cultural setting, the notion and practice of teamwork can vary. The rationale for promoting teamwork is that it creates a sense of unity and develops synergy in efforts toward task accomplishment. In some other settings, competition is emphasized. It is viewed as an indication of self-reliance and independence. Also, any prize or recognition will be given to the person who was actually the most productive. Therefore, competition is viewed as a way to energize employees, as everyone will attempt to do their best. The point here is not to build a comparative analysis between the two approaches, but to explain that any approach will fail to produce the same results across all cultures.

Problematic Facilitators: Words and Phrases

To communicate with one another, in addition to nonverbal behaviors and expressions, we heavily rely on words and phrases. Yet, as I discussed to some extent, there are some words that can become problematic because they carry more than one meaning, some of which I will review here.

Multiple Meanings of Words The word "premium" can signify a high-quality product. In non-price promotional activities, "premium" is a product offered in addition to the product intended for sale. For example, suppose you purchased a pair of shoes. With your purchase you received a container of shoe polish. The purpose for this, expectedly, is to entice customers to buy. However, in the insurance field, this term means a monthly (or periodic) payment.

There are many familiar words that have found their way into the world of technology. These words include "hardware," "software," "keyboard," "home," "journal", "mouse," and Internet "cookies."

In French "moyen" means "average," and also means "a device." For example an automobile is a "moyen" of transportation. In French, probably as in any other language, there are some words that are written almost the same way and have the same pronunciation but have completely different meanings.

- "Vers" (with a silent "s") means "toward." It also means a part of poetry.

- "Ver" means "worm."

- "Vert" (with silent "t") means green.

- "Verre" means "drinking glass."

It is interesting to note that there are words with the same spelling and pronunciation that carry different meanings depending on the context of communication. In Farsi, for example, the word "shear," can mean "milk," "lion," or "faucet."

Different Meanings of a Phrase A manager of an international subsidiary of a U.S. firm was asked to provide data showing the breakdown of individuals in that organization, meaning the number of males and females. The manager responded, "... none broken down by sex....If you must know, our problem here is with alcohol." [1]

Mr. and Mrs. Smith, a host family in Boulder, Colorado, shared this experience about a guest student. An international student, who just arrived in Boulder, was eager to try a casual and traditional American meal. Mr. and Mrs. Smith and the newcomer went to a nearby hamburger restaurant. The host wanted to order a hamburger and french fries for the guest student to try. The student politely declared that he did not eat ham, considering the tenants of his religion. Although he was assured that there was no ham in the hamburger, the guest preferred to have a chicken salad instead.

Maintaining effective communication with a person from a different culture often becomes more challenging. For example, saying, "I am sorry," in one culture may commonly mean, "I made a mistake," and in another culture it may mean "I am sorry for what has happened." The following is an illustration of such misunderstanding.

One car ran into another car that was stopped at the red traffic light. The police officer at the scene noticed that the driver of the front car, who was a Japanese man, was saying that he was sorry, meaning that he was sorry for what has happened, and not because he was at fault. But the officer misunderstood his comment and gave him a ticket.[2]

A phrase can also be used as an expression or be taken literally, which may have a different meaning. For example, in the field of human resources, this expression could be used by an employer or an interviewer, "To work here, you really need to sell yourself," meaning that one has to demonstrate capabilities pertinent to the position. Another one is, "getting up on the wrong side of bed," meaning to be in a bad mood.

There are different expressions with basically similar meanings. In Farsi, a person having "a pebble in his shoe" means the same as someone having "something up his sleeve." Both mean that this person is being cunning or is not being truthful.

Same Words but Opposite Meanings There was a time that the word "hot" could be used to refer to a thing or behavior that was out of the ordinary. Now, that meaning of the word "hot" has evolved to mean quite the opposite, "cool."

The word "burning" can mean to destroy, although contemporarily, the word "burning" is also used to signify making a copy. This term is commonly used to refer to making copies of CDs or DVDs, but it also can be used in other contexts. To this effect, one of my international students was working for an architectural firm as part of his internship program toward his graduate degree. One of his immediate superiors handed him a few legal-size documents and asked him to burn copies of them. The student associated the word "burn" with the word "destroy." Therefore, he thought that his superior wanted to completely get rid of the documents by burning them. This is exactly what he did. Later, when the superior found out about the confusion, it was too late.

The Intricacy of Communication in Cross-Cultural Settings

The potential for misunderstanding is always present among communicators. Intercultural communication, expectedly, is fertile ground for such a condition because of wider variation in perceptions, values, attitudes, the meanings assigned to words and the contexts in which exchanges of messages take place. For example, in England someone might say "I hired a car," whereas in the United States it is common to say "I rented a car." In England, someone might say, "Let's go to the cinema," which is the same as "Let's go see a movie" in the United States. Quite often, even the volume of people's voices is different from one culture to another. People in Asian countries, most notably in China and Japan, speak in a lower volume in their conversations. One of my Chinese students pointed out that the number of people living in a household in China is probably more than in most other countries. Family members sit and stand closer to each other, so a lower volume of voice is sufficient to communicate.

The point is that misunderstandings have a higher occurrence in cross-cultural settings. The real issue is how to deal with them. Recently, I have had opportunities to speak with many international CEOs. When I have asked these individuals about their biggest challenges in international settings, almost each and every one of them has directed my attention to cultural understanding or, should we say, misunderstanding. One of them pointed out that we can learn about a country's environmental conditions, level of income and economic develop-ment, legal issues pertinent to international trade, GDP, and so on, but learning about culture is a whole different phenomenon.

Below we can see a short list of areas in which misunderstanding could occur in cross-cultural settings:

- How straightforward should one be and how soon should they enter into negotiation?

- When one party waits for the other party to initiate a business offering, does it mean the first party is less eager and will therefore have an upper hand?

- Should we take off our shoes when entering a room (for negotiation)?

- Should we shake hands, bow, or both simultaneously?

- Would it be proper to shake hands with someone of another gender?

- Is it proper to exchange gifts?

- What gift and what color would be proper?

- What should be the monetary value of the gift? An inexpensive gift could be offensive, but an expensive one might imply bribery.

- Can we rely on a firm handshake as a binding contract, or must a written document be signed?

- Does a signed contract mean the end of negotiation or will it continue afterward as it happens in some countries?

- What is the meaning of "yes?" Does it mean "I agree," or simply mean "I heard you?"

Such a list seems to be endless, so one can imagine the intricacies of cross-cultural communication in both business and interpersonal settings.

Tackling Communication in Cross-Cultural Settings

The remainder of this chapter provides guidelines to alleviate misunderstanding in intercultural environments.

Active Listening I do not know of any culture or nationality that underestimates the critical role of active listening. In most cases, one would prefer to talk rather than listen. Therefore, continual listening to another individual can become boring, particularly when there is no common interest in the topic. However, active listening has several beneficial outcomes. It indicates intelligence, the ability to concentrate, and concern for the other party and what is being said. Such caring is commonly contagious, and the other party tends to reciprocate and listen as well. Such reciprocal listening fosters friendship and will pave the road to mutual cultural understanding.

Culture-Gap Analysis When planning to interact with people of different cultural backgrounds, there are two features that must be taken into account. First, learn about that culture as much as you reasonably can beforehand. This can be done by reading relevant books and articles, and by going through specific cultural training programs. If you are becoming an expatriate, chances are that your company will facilitate such programs for you. Moreover, when possible, listen to the pertinent radio stations and watch television aired from that county. This way, one can learn about the way residents interact and communicate.

Second, examine your own ability and willingness to be within a society of different values, customs, and attitudes. In many societies, for example, bribery is ethically, socially, and legally forbidden, whereas in some other societies it is a common practice, but in a concealed way. Yet, there are other societies, where bribery, extortion, or "lubrication" are not only permitted but are the way of life. That can happen when bureaucrats' salaries are considerably less than adequate and they have to rely on such secondary income. Interestingly enough, these incomes must be reported to the government for the purpose of income tax. Imagine an expatriate who is assigned to live in that social environment with a conviction that bribery and similar practices are wrong.

Third, utilize self-experiential learning outcomes by living in a host country as a device for future international missions. An expatriate can amass considerable amounts of experience after the completion of a first mission. This practical, or hands-on, experience can be quite beneficial for the upcoming assigned missions. It is similar to learning foreign languages; once an individual learns one language, and then learning another becomes easier.

Help from Translators In an international negotiation process or for writing up a formal business contract, it is important to have a qualified translator. A translator can help ensure that each of the involved parties has a clear understanding of each specification of the negotiation. Translation is a thorny task because of the possibility of mistranslation of a word or a sentence. It is therefore advisable to rely on something known as "back translation." Via this process, a contract written, for example, in Chinese, will be translated to English. Then, what has been translated to English will be translated back to Chinese. If the translation and back translation are similar, then translation is effective.

The way people react or perceive a sentence can also make the task of translation more complicated. Often, we see owners' manuals for equipment with terms such as "DO NOT." In some cultures, such instructions would be viewed as authoritarian, and as a result the instruction would be ignored or the product returned to the store for a refund. An alternative in this case would be a translation such as "Would you please." The dilemma is should a translation be the exact interpretation of the original written instruction, or should the translation be changed somewhat to better fit a given cultural perception?

The Wall Street Journal noted that faulty translations can have many adverse consequences, including the loss of human lives. An operator manual for a cement mixer was translated with an error that caused a pile of cement to fall on a worker in the Middle East.[3]

Final Notes

Understandingly, through working and interacting with people of different cultural backgrounds, one will be faced with potential misunderstandings and ambiguity, but this can be an illuminating learning experience that cannot be acquired when working with people of one's own society with similar customs, language, and modes of behavior. Open-mindedness, adaptability, and appreciation of cultural variations are essential for a successful experience in the multicultural arena.

ENDNOTES

1. An incident of misunderstanding in Lima, Peru by Jack L. Ottiker in Roger E. Axtell, *The Do's and Taboos of International Trade: a Small Business Primer,* Revised ed. (New York: John Wiley & Sons, 1994), p. 224.

2. Jennifer J. Labbs, "Hotels Train to Help Japanese Guests," *Personnel Journal,* September 1994, p.29.

3. G. Christian Hill, "Language for Profit: More Firms Turn to Translation Experts to Avoid Costly, Embarrassing Mistakes," *The Wall Street Journal,* January 13, 1977, p. 34.

RECOMMENDED READING

John W. Santrock. Human Adjustment. New York: McGraw Hill Company, 2006.

Gary Dessler. *Human Resource Management.* Upper Saddle River, NJ: Pearson Prentice Hall, 2005.

Carl Rodrigues. *International Management: A Cultural Approach.* Cincinnati: South Western College Publishing Thomas Learning, 2001.

Richard W. Brislin, *Cross-Cultural Encounters.* New York: Pergamon Press, 1982.

Ronald B. Adler and Neil Towne. *Looking Out/ Looking In: Interpersonal Communication.* Fort Worth, TX: Harcourt Brace College Publisher, 1993.

Index

A B

advertising, 14, 65, 90-91, 93, 95, 97-98
acronyms, 31, 39, 41
ambiguity, 17, 45-47, 53, 59-60, 79, 90, 137
America Express, 65
American market, 91-92
American(s), 35, 51, 91-92, 105, 110, 113-114
Angel, Pamela A., 76
Archer, Dave, 110, 120
Austria, 27-28
Avianca, 36, 50
Axtell, Roger E., 14, 138
bargaining, 107, 110
Brazil, 4
bribery, 116, 134, 136
Brislin, Richard W., 138

C

Canada, 3, 34, 110
Canary Islands, 37
ceremonial
        communication, 10
        proposition, 38
China, 1, 4, 25, 28, 110, 115, 120, 133
colloquialisms, 31, 39, 51
Colombia, 36
commercials, 89, 92-93, 95
communication, 5, 6, 10, 13, 21-23, 37, 49, 52, 68, 101-102, 152

breakdowns, 3, 17
face-to-face, 6-7
effective, 3, 13, 18, 131
interpersonal, 7-8, 19, 21-22, 37
nonverbal, 3, 17, 19, 21, 23-24, 35-36
verbal, 3, 17, 19, 21, 23-24, 35-36
communication, organizational, 10
downward, 10, 62, 71
lateral, 10
upward, 10, 71
communication, human, 3
individual perspective, 4-5
national perspective, 3
organizational perspective, 3
competition, 31, 80, 92, 117, 121, 129
complex organizations, 52, 75
conflict, 10, 109, 121, 127-128
confiscation, 116
creative ambiguity, 59
cross-cultural settings, 100, 132-135, 138
customer's loyalty, 84, 107

D

De Bono, Edward, 101, 120
decision-making process, 93
centralized, 93
decentralized, 93
decode, 6, 11
demand, 60, 62, 79
diversity, 44, 127
Drucker, Peter F., 23, 29

E

economic integration, 3
Electrolux, 91
encoding, 17
England, 90-91, 114, 133
euphemism, 29
Europe, 72, 92-93, 114
European Free Trade Association (EFTA), 3
expropriation, 116
extortion, 116, 136
eye contact, 25, 35

F

facial expressions (in communication), 23-25, 110
Federal Trade Commission, the (FTC), 93
feedback, 7, 10
fingers (in communication), 25
"Five Cs", approach to organizational relationships, 67-68
        coaching, 68
        commitment, 69
        communication, 68
        connectivity, 68
        cooperation, 68-69
Florida, Richard, 69, 76
foreign direct investment, 115
France, 40, 93, 112
Free Trade Area (FTA), 3
foreign products, 116

G

General Motors (GM), 4, 91
Germans, 113
Gillespie, Kate, 97
Glover, Katherine, M., 110,120
Golghaber, Gerald M., 50
Goodnight, Jim, 76, 88
green marketing, 27
groupthink, 56-57
guidance, 10, 26

H

Hakim, 9
halo effect, 54-55
handshakes, 23, 112
Hennessy, H. David, 97
hidden agenda, 89
Hill, Christian G., 138

I

Iceland, 3
income, 102, 126
      per capita 5, 95, 118
      supplemental, 116
      level, 127, 133
      secondary, 136
India, 4, 24
instrumentality, 109-110
Iran, 114
Italians, 114
Italy, 27, 90, 93

J

Japan, 4, 25, 92, 110, 113-114, 131, 133
Japanese, 92, 113-114, 131, 138
jargons, 31, 39, 40
Jeannet, Jean-Pierre, 97
job description, 4, 76
joint-venture agreements, 113, 115
Jones, Thomas O., 66, 76

K L

Kennedy International Airport, 36
KLM, 37
Kitcatt Nohr, 90
Kodak, 41
Labbs, Jennifer J., 138
Lane, Ronald, W., 93, 97
leadership, 75, 121, 127-128
Liechtenstein, 3
listening, 2, 64, 81, 111, 135
literacy, level of, 95-96
LL Bean, 65
lubrication, 116, 136

M

Magnuson, Ed, 50
management effectiveness, 22, 69
    comfort zone, 22, 70-71, 73
    macroenvironment, 70-71
    microenvironment, 70, 73
marketing, 80-81, 97
    ambiguity, 79, 90
    decisions, 95, 122

direct, 95
investment, 96
messages, 92
research, 82, 117
techniques, 84
volume, 86
misunderstanding(s), 2-3, 13, 17-21, 23-26, 28, 31-33, 36-39, 41-49, 54, 57, 61-63, 66, 84, 86, 89-91, 96-100, 106, 109, 111, 113, 115, 118, 121-122, 125, 127, 131-134, 137-138
marketing evolution in the United States, 79, 83
    embryonic, 80, 83
    expansive, 80, 83
    growth, 80, 83
    presaturation, 81, 83
    saturation, 82-83
Maslow, A. H., 14
message(s), 10, 23-24, 28. 87, 89, 92-93, 111, 133
Mexico, 3, 91, 110
Middle-East, the, 27, 112, 137
misleading pricing, 87
misleading volume, 84
Moyers, Bill, 29

N

name, (use of) first and last, 113
negotiation, 13, 18, 96, 99-100
    mono-locus approach, 100
    poly-locus approach, 102
New York, 36
Newstrom, John W., 19
nodding, 24
noise, 7
nonverbal communication, 2, 13, 17, 21, 23-24, 35-36
nonverbal cues, 28, 111

Nordstrom, 65, 84
North America, 24, 92
North American Free Trade Agreement (NAFTA), 3
Norway, 3
nudity, 93

O P

organization(s), 3, 52, 54, 58, 70, 72-73, 75, 94, 113, 127-128
Pakistan, 26, 27, 114
Pan American airlines, 37
perception, 22, 38, 42, 55-56, 91, 116, 133, 137
Peru, 35
playing politics, 58
political stability, 116
product(s), 46, 66-68, 71, 80, 82, 84-85, 88-89, 90-93, 95, 116-117, 129, 137
production, 4, 27, 46-47, 61, 67, 80
productivity, 59, 82, 129
projection, 55
protocol(s), 3, 42, 44, 99, 111, 114, 118

Q R

quotas, 3, 119
relationship(s), 21, 59, 67-68, 100, 102, 109-110, 123
response, 6-7, 11, 19, 24, 38, 45, 55, 59, 94, 111, 113, 125
research, 82, 95, 117
      primary, 117
      secondary, 117-118
Ricks, David A., 36, 50
Ritz Carlton, 65
Russell, Thomas, J., 93, 97

S

SAS, 69
sales, 67, 84-85, 87-88, 91, 95
Sasser, Jr., W. Earl, 66, 76
satisfaction, 102, 104, 105
      customer, 63-67, 69, 75
      employee, 19, 69
Saudi Arabia, 114
Scandinavian countries, 70, 110, 115
Schermerhorn, Jr., John R., 76
Shah, Aziz, 14
self-misunderstanding, 121-126
sentence(s), 48, 136-137
signature, 81, 112
South America, 114
South Korea, 4
success, meaning of, 121, 127
supply, 79-81, 83
Switzerland, 3, 27, 113-114

T

tariff(s), 3, 118
teamwork, 68, 72-73, 121, 127, 129
Tenerife Airport, 37
terminality109-110
Timotei Shampoo, 91
Toyota, 4
translation, 116, 136-137
translator, 136

U

United Motor Manufacturing, Inc., the, 4
United States, the, 1, 3, 26, 33-34, 72, 79, 82-83, 92, 104, 107, 112-114, 133
understanding, 9, 17-19, 22, 37, 46, 49, 65, 68, 75, 100, 121, 133, 137

V W X Y Z

verbal, 2, 13, 17, 19-21, 23, 28, 31-32, 35-36, 54, 111
voice, volume of, 133
Western European market, 91
wholly owned subsidiary, 115
words
        multiple meanings of, 129
        opposite meanings of, 132
World Bank, 14
writing dates, documents and letters,113
Xerox, 65, 66
Ybarra, Oscar, 11, 14
zero-sum game, 100

About the Author

Professor Bagher Fardanesh earned his B.S. in Business Administration, M.A. in Public Administration, and Ph.D. in Higher Education from the University of Colorado at Boulder. Having a multidisciplinary academic background, he has been teaching a range of undergraduate and graduate courses, including international business, international management, and strategic management. Professor Fardanesh has more than twenty-five years teaching experience in the United States and overseas

He is the founder of Farco International, a management consulting firm in Boulder, Colorado, and served as the chair of a World Affairs Conference at the University of Colorado. He has given numerous seminars and conducted management consulting in the United States, Canada, the Middle East, and Western Europe. In his professional practice, he has served organizations such as the international operations of General Motors, Noranda Centre de Technologie in Quebec, the Johns Hopkins University in Baltimore, Maryland Workforce Development Association, Lockheed Martin, and World Trade Center Institute. Dr. Fardanesh is on the review panel for selected marketing and management textbooks of the McGraw Hill and Irwin publishing company.

Dr. Fardanesh is a world traveler who has lived in several countries in the Middle East and Western Europe, as well as in the United States and Canada. He is multi-lingual with an in-depth appreciation and understanding of multicultural settings.